THE
TAMING
OF THE
SHREW

.THE NEW.
FOLGER LIBRARY
SHAKESPEARE

THE
TAMING
OF THE
SHREW

BY

WILLIAM SHAKESPEARE

WASHINGTON SQUARE PRESS

New York   London   Toronto   Sydney   Singapore

A Washington Square Press Publication
1230 Avenue of the Americas, New York, NY 10020

ISBN: 0-7434-5297-6

Washington Square Press New Folger Library Hardcover Edition
November 2002

10 9 8 7 6 5 4 3 2 1

For information regarding special discounts for bulk purchases,
please contact Simon & Schuster Special Sales at 1-800-456-6798
or business@simonandschuster.com

Printed in the U.S.A.

From the Director of the Library

For over thirty-five years, the Folger Library General Reader's Shakespeare has provided accurate and accessible texts of the plays and poems to students, teachers, and hundreds of thousands of other interested readers. Today, in an age often impatient with the past, the passion for Shakespeare continues to grow. No author speaks more powerfully to the human condition, in all its variety, than this actor/playwright from a minor sixteenth-century English village.

Over three decades, much has changed in the way Shakespeare's works are edited, performed, studied, and taught. It is time to replace the earlier Folger Shakespeare with an entirely new version, one that incorporates the best and most current thinking concerning both the texts and their interpretation. Professors Barbara Mowat and Paul Werstine are uniquely qualified to produce this New Folger Shakespeare for a new generation of readers. The Library is grateful for the learning, clarity, and imagination they have brought to this ambitious project.

Werner Gundersheimer,
Director of the Folger Shakespeare Library
from 1984 to 2002

Contents

Editors' Preface

In recent years, ways of dealing with Shakespeare's texts
and with the interpretation of his plays have been
undergoing significant change. This edition, while re-
taining many of the features that have always made the
Folger Shakespeare so attractive to the general reader, at
the same time reflects these current ways of thinking
about Shakespeare. For example, modern readers, actors, and teachers have become interested in the differences between, on the one hand, the early forms in
which Shakespeare's plays were first published and, on
the other hand, the forms in which editors through the
centuries have presented them. In response to this
interest, we have based our edition on what we consider
the best early printed version of a particular play (explaining our rationale in a section called "An Introduction to This Text") and have marked our changes in the
text—unobtrusively, we hope, but in such a way that the
curious reader can be aware that a change has been
made and can consult the "Textual Notes" to discover
what appeared in the early printed version.

Current ways of looking at the plays are reflected in
our brief introductions, in many of the commentary
notes, in the annotated lists of "Further Reading," and
especially in each play's "Modern Perspective," an essay
written by an outstanding scholar who brings to the
reader his or her fresh assessment of the play in the light
of today's interests and concerns.

As in the Folger Library General Reader's Shakespeare, which this edition replaces, we include explana-
tory notes designed to help make Shakespeare's language clearer to a modern reader, and we place the

notes on the page facing the text that they explain. We also follow the earlier edition in including illustrations —of objects, of clothing, of mythological figures—from books and manuscripts in the Folger Library collection. We provide fresh accounts of the life of Shakespeare, of the publishing of his plays, and of the theaters in which his plays were performed, as well as an introduction to the text itself. We also include a section called "Reading Shakespeare's Language," in which we try to help readers learn to "break the code" of Elizabethan poetic language.

For each section of each volume, we are indebted to a host of generous experts and fellow scholars. The "Reading Shakespeare's Language" sections, for example, could not have been written had not Arthur King, of Brigham Young University, and Randal Robinson, author of *Unlocking Shakespeare's Language,* led the way in untangling Shakespearean language puzzles and shared their insights and methodologies generously with us. "Shakespeare's Life" profited by the careful reading given it by S. Schoenbaum, "Shakespeare's Theater" was read and strengthened by Andrew Gurr and John Astington, and "The Publication of Shakespeare's Plays" is indebted to the comments of Peter W. M. Blayney. We, as editors, take sole responsibility for any errors in our editions.

We are grateful to the authors of the "Modern Perspectives," to Leeds Barroll and David Bevington for their generous encouragement, to the Huntington and Newberry Libraries for fellowship support, to King's College for the grants it has provided to Paul Werstine, to the Social Sciences and Humanities Research Council of Canada, which provided him with a Research Time Stipend for 1990–91, and to the Folger Institute's Center for Shakespeare Studies for its fortuitous sponsorship of a workshop on "Shakespeare's Texts for Students and

Teachers" (funded by the National Endowment for the Humanities and led by Richard Knowles of the University of Wisconsin), a workshop from which we learned an enormous amount about what is wanted by college and high-school teachers of Shakespeare today.

Our biggest debt is to the Folger Shakespeare Library: to Werner Gundersheimer, Director of the Library, who has made possible our edition; to Jean Miller, the Library's Art Curator, who combed the Library holdings for illustrations, and to Julie Ainsworth, Head of the Photography Department, who carefully photographed them; to Peggy O'Brien, Director of Education, who gave us expert advice about the needs being expressed by Shakespeare teachers and students (and to Martha Christian and other "master teachers" who used our texts in manuscript in their classrooms); to the staff of the Academic Programs Division, especially Paul Menzer (who drafted "Further Reading" material), Mary Tonkinson, Lena Cowen Orlin, Molly Haws, and Jessica Hymowitz; and, finally, to the staff of the Library Reading Room, whose patience and support have been invaluable.

Barbara A. Mowat and Paul Werstine

THE
Taming of the Shrew.

Actus primus. Scœna Prima.

Enter Begger and Hoftes, Chriftophero Sly.

Begger.

Le pheeze you infaith.

Hoft. A paire of ftockes you rogue.

Beg. Y'are a baggage, the *Slies* are no Rogues. Looke in the Chronicles, we came in with *Richard Conqueror*: therefore *Paucas pallabris*, let the world flide: Seffa.

Hoft. You will not pay for the glaffes you haue burft?

Beg. No, not a deniere: go by S. *Ieronimie*, goe to thy cold bed, and warme thee.

Hoft. I know my remedie, I muft go fetch the Head-borough.

Beg. Third, or fourth, or fift Borough, Ile anfwere him by Law. Ile not budge an inch boy: Let him come, and kindly.   *Falles afleepe.*

Winde hornes. Enter a Lord from hunting, with his traine.

Lo. Huntfman I charge thee, tender wel my hounds, Brach *Meriman*, the poore Curre is imboft, And couple *Clowder* with the deepe-mouth'd brach, Saw'ft thou not boy how *Siluer* made it good At the hedge corner, in the couldeft fault, I would not loofe the dogge for twentie pound.

Huntf. Why *Belman* is as good as he my Lord, He cried vpon it at the meereft loffe, And twice to day pick'd out the dulleft fent, Truft me, I take him for the better dogge.

Lord. Thou art a Foole, if *Eccho* were as fleete, I would efteeme him worth a dozen fuch: But fup them well, and looke vnto them all, To morrow I intend to hunt againe.

Huntf. I will my Lord.

Lord. What's heere? One dead, or drunke? See doth he breath?

2.Hun. He breath's my Lord. Were he not warm'd with Ale, this were a bed but cold to fleepe fo foundly.

Lord. Oh monftrous beaft, how like a fwine he lyes. Grim death, how foule and loathfome is thine image: Sirs, I will practife on this drunken man. What thinke you, if he were conuey'd to bed, Wrap'd in fweet cloathes: Rings put vpon his fingers: A moft delicious banquet by his bed, And braue attendants neere him when he wakes, Would not the begger then forget himfelfe?

1.Hun. Beleeue me Lord, I thinke he cannot choofe.

2.H. It would feeme ftrange vnto him when he wak'd

Lord. Euen as a flatt'ring dreame, or worthleffe fancie.

Then take him vp, and mannage well the ieft: Carrie him gently to my faireft Chamber, And hang it round with all my wanton pictures: Balme his foule head in warme diftilled waters, And burne fweet Wood to make the Lodging fweete: Procure me Muficke readie when he wakes, To make a dulcet and a heauenly found: And if he chance to fpeake, be readie ftraight (And with a lowe fubmiffiue reuerence) Say, what is it your Honor will command: Let one attend him with a filuer Bafon Full of Rofe-water, and beftrew'd with Flowers, Another beare the Ewer: the third a Diaper, And fay wilt pleafe your Lordfhip coole your hands. Some one be readie with a coftly fuite, And aske him what apparrel he will weare: Another tell him of his Hounds and Horfe, And that his Ladie mournes at his difeafe, Perfwade him that he hath bin Lunaticke, And when he fayes he is, fay that he dreames, For he is nothing but a mightie Lord: This do, and do it kindly, gentle firs, It wil be paftime paffing excellent, If it be husbanded with modeftie.

1.Huntf. My Lord I warrant you we wil play our part As he fhall thinke by our true diligence He is no leffe then what we fay he is.

Lord. Take him vp gently, and to bed with him, And each one to his office when he wakes.

Sound trumpets.

Sirrah, go fee what Trumpet 'tis that founds, Belike fome Noble Gentleman that meanes (Trauelling fome iourney) to repofe him heere.

Enter Seruingman.

How now? who is it?

Ser. An't pleafe your Honor, Players That offer feruice to your Lordfhip.

Enter Players.

Lord. Bid them come neere: Now felowes, you are welcome.

Players. We thanke your Honor.

Lord. Do you intend to ftay with me to night?

2.Player. So pleafe your Lordfhippe to accept our dutie.

Lord. With all my heart. This fellow I remember, Since once he plaide a Farmers eldeft fonne, 'Twas where you woo'd the Gentlewoman fo well: I haue forgot your name: but fure that part

W 2

Shakespeare's
The Taming of the Shrew

Love and marriage are the concerns of Shakespeare's *The Taming of the Shrew*. The play offers us some strikingly different models of the process of attracting and choosing a mate and then coming to terms with the mate one has chosen. Some of these models may still seem attractive to us, some not. Lucentio's courtship of and marriage to Bianca are prompted by his idealized love of an apparently ideal woman. When she first appears, Bianca is silent and perfectly obedient to her father. Lucentio then speaks of her as if she were a goddess come to earth. Because her father denies all men the opportunity openly to court Bianca, Lucentio spontaneously throws off his social status as a gentleman in order to disguise himself as a lowly tutor, the only kind of man that Bianca's father, Baptista, will let near her. All that matters to Lucentio is winning Bianca's heart. To marry her—even in secret and in shared defiance of her father—is surely, he believes, to be happy.

An alternative style of wooing adopted by Petruchio in quest of Katherine is notably free of idealism. Petruchio is concerned with money. He takes money from all Bianca's suitors for wooing her older sister, Katherine, who, Baptista has dictated, must be married before Bianca. When Petruchio comes to see Katherine, he first arranges with her father the dowry to be acquired by marrying her. Assured of the money, Petruchio is ready to marry Katherine even against her will. Katherine is the shrew named in the play's title; and, according to all

"Fair Padua, nursery of arts."

From Pietro Bertelli, *Theatrum vrbium Italicarum . . .* (1599).

the men but Petruchio, her bad temper denies her the status of "ideal woman" accorded Bianca by Lucentio. Yet by the end of the play, Katherine, whether she has been tamed or not, certainly acts much changed. Petruchio then claims to have the more successful marriage. But is the marriage of Petruchio and Katherine a superior match—have they truly learned to love each other?—or is it based on terror and deception?

This question about Katherine and Petruchio is only one of the questions this play raises for us. How are we to respond to Kate's speech at the end of the play, with its celebration of the wife's subordinate position? What does it mean that Bianca, the "ideal" woman, at the end seems unpleasant and bad-tempered, now that she is married? How should we respond to the process by which Petruchio "tames" Kate? As with so many of Shakespeare's plays, how one answers these questions has a lot to do with one's own basic beliefs—here, one's beliefs about men and women, about love and marriage.

After you have read *The Taming of the Shrew*, we invite you to turn to the discussion of the play printed in the back of this book and entitled "A Modern Perspective," written by Professor Karen Newman of Brown University.

Reading Shakespeare's Language

For many people today, reading Shakespeare's language can be a problem—but it is a problem that can be solved. Those who have studied Latin (or even French or German or Spanish) and those who are used to reading poetry, will have little difficulty understanding the language of Shakespeare's poetic drama. Others, though, need to develop the skills of untangling unusual sentence structures and of recognizing and understanding poetic compressions, omissions, and wordplay. And even those skilled in reading unusual sentence structures may have occasional trouble with Shakespeare's words. Four hundred years of "static" intervene between his speaking and our hearing. Most of his immense vocabulary is still in use, but a few of his words are not, and, worse, some of his words now have meanings quite different from those they had in the sixteenth century. In the theater, most of these difficulties are solved for us by actors who study the language and articulate it for us so that the essential meaning is heard—or, when combined with stage action, is at least *felt*. When reading on one's own, one must do what each actor does: go over the lines (often with a dictionary close at hand) until the puzzles are solved and the lines yield up their poetry and the characters speak in words and phrases that are, suddenly, rewarding and wonderfully memorable.

Shakespeare's Words

As you begin to read the opening scenes of a play by Shakespeare, you may notice occasional unfamiliar words. Some are unfamiliar simply because we no longer use them. In the opening scenes of *The Taming of the Shrew*, for example, you will find the words *feeze you* (i.e., fix you, do for you), *an* (i.e., if), *bestraught* (i.e., distracted), and *iwis* (i.e., certainly). Words of this kind are explained in notes to the text and will become familiar the more of Shakespeare's plays you read.

Some words are strange not because of the "static" introduced by changes in language over the past centuries but because these are words that Shakespeare is using to build a dramatic world that has its own space and time. *The Taming of the Shrew* is a particularly complicated example of Shakespeare's construction of a dramatic world in that he creates one world in what we call the "Induction"—a world inhabited by an English beggar and an English lord and his attendants—and then creates a second, Italian, world for the main body of the play. In the Induction we find *rogues, stocks,* and *headboroughs,* as well as references to deep-mouthed brachs, wanton pictures, obeisances, and embracements. In the opening scenes of the main body of the play, the setting in Italy and the story's focus on wooing are created through repeated references to Padua, to Lombardy, to Pisa, to dowries, to Ovid, to poesy, and to Minerva, and through such Italian phrases as *Mi perdonato* and *basta.* These "local" references create the Padua that Kate, Petruchio, Lucentio, and Bianca inhabit and will become increasingly familiar to you as you get further into the play.

In *The Taming of the Shrew,* as in all of Shakespeare's writing, the most problematic words are those that we still use but that we use with a different meaning. In the opening scenes of *The Taming of the Shrew,* for example, the word *heavy* has the meaning of "distressing," the word *envious* is used where we would say "malicious," *brave* where we would say "splendid," *idle* where we would say "silly," and *curst* where we would say "bad-tempered." Such words will be explained in the notes to the text, but they, too, will become familiar as you continue to read Shakespeare's language.

Shakespeare's Sentences

In an English sentence, meaning is quite dependent on the place given each word. "The dog bit the boy" and

"The boy bit the dog" mean very different things, even though the individual words are the same. Because English places such importance on the positions of words in sentences, on the way words are arranged, unusual arrangements can puzzle a reader. Shakespeare frequently shifts his sentences away from "normal" English arrangements—often to create the rhythm he seeks, sometimes to use a line's poetic rhythm to emphasize a particular word, sometimes to give a character his or her own speech patterns or to allow the character to speak in a special way. Again, when we attend a good performance of the play, the actors will have worked out the sentence structures and will articulate the sentences so that the meaning is clear. In reading for yourself, do as the actor does. That is, when you become puzzled by a character's speech, check to see if words are being presented in an unusual sequence.

Look first for the placement of subject and verb. Shakespeare often places the verb before the subject (e.g., instead of "He goes," we find "Goes he"). In the Induction to *The Taming of the Shrew*, we find such a construction when Christopher Sly is told "Hence comes it that your kindred shuns your house" (In.2.28) (instead of "Hence it comes that . . . "); Hortensio uses this same kind of construction when, at 1.1.87–88, he says, "*Sorry am I* that our goodwill effects /Bianca's grief." Such inversions rarely cause much confusion. More problematic is Shakespeare's frequent placing of the object before the subject and verb (e.g., instead of "I hit him," we might find "Him I hit"). Tranio's "Music and poesy use to quicken you" (1.1.36) is an example of such an inversion (the normal order would be "Use music and poesy . . . "), as are Baptista's "Schoolmasters will I keep" (1.1.96), Lucentio's "Vincentio's son . . . /It shall become" (1.1.14–15), and Petruchio's "Crowns in my purse I have" (1.2.58). Occasionally in

The Taming of the Shrew (which is one of Shakespeare's very early plays), the subject-verb-object sequencing is unusually contorted, as in Baptista's "For how I firmly am resolved you know" (1.1.49, where the normal sentence order would be: "For you know how I am firmly resolved"). Here, and elsewhere, the inversions serve primarily to create regular iambic pentameter lines.

Inversions are not the only unusual sentence structures in Shakespeare's language. Often in his sentences words that would normally appear together are separated from each other. (Again, this is often done to create a particular rhythm or to stress a particular word.) Take, for example, Hortensio's "Her only fault, and that is faults enough, / Is that she is intolerable curst" (1.2.89–90); here the phrase "and that is faults enough" separates the noun ("fault") from its verb ("Is"). Or take Lucentio's lines that begin at 1.1.153, "*I found* the effect of love-in-idleness, / *And* now in plainness *do confess to thee* / That art to me as secret and as dear / As Anna to the Queen of Carthage was: / Tranio, *I burn, I pine! I perish, Tranio*." Here the normal construction "I found . . . and do confess to thee . . . : I burn, I pine" is interrupted by the insertion of a series of phrases and clauses. In order to create for yourself sentences that seem more like the English of everyday speech, you may wish to rearrange the words, putting together the word clusters ("her fault is that," "do confess to thee: I burn, I pine"). You will usually find that the sentence will gain in clarity but will lose its rhythm or shift its emphasis.

Locating and rearranging words that "belong together" is especially necessary in passages that separate subjects from verbs and verbs from objects by long delaying or expanding interruptions. Tranio uses such an interrupted construction when he says to Lucentio at 1.1.217–22:

> In brief, sir, *sith it your pleasure is,*
> *And I am tied to be obedient*
> (For so your father charged me at our parting:
> "Be serviceable to my son," quoth he,
> Although I think 'twas in another sense),
> *I am content to be Lucentio.*

In some plays (*Hamlet,* for instance), long interrupted sentences are used to catch the audience up in the narrative or are used as a characterizing device. In *The Taming of the Shrew,* the interruptions are more often simply extra bits of detail. Lucentio's opening speech in 1.1, for instance, includes descriptive details for almost every city or person named.

> Tranio, since for [i.e., because of] the great desire I
>   had
> To see fair Padua, *nursery of arts,*
> I am arrived for [i.e., have arrived in] fruitful
>   Lombardy,
> *The pleasant garden of great Italy,*
> And by my father's love and leave am armed
> With his goodwill and thy good company.
> My trusty servant *well approved in all,*
> Here let us breathe [i.e., remain] and haply institute
> A course of learning and ingenious studies.
> Pisa, *renownèd for grave citizens,*
> Gave me my being, and my father first,
> *A merchant of great traffic through the world,*
> Vincentio, *come of the Bentivolii.*
> Vincentio's son, *brought up in Florence,*
> It shall become to serve all hopes conceived
> To deck his fortune with his virtuous deeds.

Such descriptive details lengthen the sentences and, in combination with such inversions as "Vincentio's son

. . . It shall become," give the verse a formal quality that marks it off both from the play's prose passages and from the much simpler and more straightforward verse of the Induction.

In several passages in *The Taming of the Shrew*, Shakespeare not only interrupts with details, but piles up detail to create extraordinary speeches (see, for example, the description of Petruchio's wedding clothes and his horse [3.2.42–62] and the description of the wedding itself [3.2.160–67]). Such speeches are hard to appreciate when read silently (especially since so many of the words he selects here are no longer in our vocabularies), but come wonderfully alive as grotesque, farcical verbal "riffs" when read aloud.

Shakespearean Wordplay

Shakespeare plays with language so often and so variously that entire books are written on the topic. Here we will mention only two kinds of wordplay, puns and metaphors. A pun is a play on words that sound the same but that have different meanings. In *The Taming of the Shrew* the scene that introduces us to Petruchio includes a long argument between Petruchio and his servant Grumio (1.2.5–21, 38–44) that turns on the word *knock* and the phrase *knock me*, by which Petruchio means "knock for me [on the gate]," but which Grumio interprets as "hit me." In 1.1, when Kate enters she says to Baptista, "I pray you, sir, is it your will / To make a stale [i.e., laughingstock] of me amongst these mates?" *Mates* here means "fellows." Hortensio replies with " 'Mates,' maid? How mean you that? No mates for you / Unless you were of gentler, milder mold," where *mates* means "husbands." The first scene between Kate and Petruchio (2.1.190–293) is built around a whole series of puns, beginning with puns on the name Kate (delicacies are known as "cates") and including puns on *sounded, movables, bear, light, take, crest, crab, arms,* and *tale/tail.* (In the glosses to this text, puns are often indicated by numbered meanings, e.g., *crab* [at 2.1.243] is glossed as "(1) crab apple; (2) sour-faced person.") In all of Shakespeare's plays, one must stay alert to the sounds of words and to the possibility of double meanings. In *The Taming of the Shrew,* many scenes are funny only if we hear the puns.

A metaphor is a play on words in which one object or idea is expressed as if it were something else, something with which it shares common features. *The Taming of the Shrew* is not rich in metaphoric language, but at one point, when Petruchio describes his method of "taming" Kate (at 4.1.190–96), he uses metaphor in a powerful and significant way:

> My falcon now is sharp and passing empty,
> And, till she stoop, she must not be full-gorged,
> For then she never looks upon her lure.
> Another way I have to man my haggard,
> To make her come and know her keeper's call.
> That is, to watch her, as we watch these kites
> That bate and beat and will not be obedient.

Here, in an extended metaphor, Kate is a falcon being tamed by its master, a "haggard" (i.e., a female hawk) being "manned," being made to "stoop." The language is taken from manuals for the training of hawks and the metaphor works out in careful detail Petruchio's image of himself as trainer and Kate as the hawk he is taming.

Implied Stage Action

Finally, in reading Shakespeare's plays you should always remember that what you are reading is a performance script. The dialogue is written to be spoken by actors who, at the same time, are moving, gesturing, picking up objects, weeping, shaking their fists. Some stage action is described in what are called "stage directions"; some is suggested within the dialogue itself. Learn to be alert to such signals as you stage the play in your imagination. When, in *The Taming of the Shrew* 1.1 212–13, Lucentio says, "Tranio, at once / Uncase thee. Take my colored hat and cloak," it is clear, from later dialogue in the scene, that they here exchange clothes; in 1.2.28, when Hortensio says, "Rise, Grumio, rise," it is equally clear that at some previous point Grumio has fallen. At several places in *The Taming of the Shrew*, signals to the reader are not quite so clear. When, after Kate and Petruchio's first meeting, Petruchio claims, untruthfully, that he and she have fallen in love and agreed to marry, and he says (2.1.333) "Give me thy hand, Kate," it is not at all clear that she does as he asks; nor do we know exactly what should happen a few lines later when her father says, "Give me your hands." Since he then says to Petruchio, "'Tis a match," we can assume that Petruchio, at least, gives Baptista his hand, but the actress playing Katherine—and you as a reader —must decide whether Katherine allows him to join their hands or refuses to do so. Even more interesting challenges are offered by the final scene of the play, where Katherine, having spoken eloquently about the proper duties of a wife, concludes her speech by saying to the other women: "place your hands below your husband's foot; / In token of which duty, if he please, / My hand is ready, may it do him ease" (5.2.193–95).

Katherine may here stoop and place her hand under Petruchio's foot—this is the case in many productions. If she does, the picture of her subjugation (or her happy acceptance of her new role) is quite different than if she merely offers to do so. The text leaves open interesting possibilities for staging this moment.

It is immensely rewarding to work carefully with Shakespeare's language so that the words, the sentences, the wordplay, and the implied stage action all become clear—as readers for the past four centuries have discovered. It may be more pleasurable to attend a good performance of a play—though not everyone has thought so. But the joy of being able to stage one of Shakespeare's plays in one's imagination, to return to passages that continue to yield further meanings (or further questions) the more one reads them—these are pleasures that, for many, rival (or at least augment) those of the performed text, and certainly make it worth considerable effort to "break the code" of Elizabethan poetic drama and let free the remarkable language that makes up a Shakespeare text.

Shakespeare's Life

Surviving documents that give us glimpses into the life of William Shakespeare show us a playwright, poet, and actor who grew up in the market town of Stratford-upon-Avon, spent his professional life in London, and returned to Stratford a wealthy landowner. He was born in April 1564, died in April 1616, and is buried inside the chancel of Holy Trinity Church in Stratford.

We wish we could know more about the life of the world's greatest dramatist. His plays and poems are

testaments to his wide reading—especially to his knowledge of Virgil, Ovid, Plutarch, Holinshed's *Chronicles*,
and the Bible—and to his mastery of the English
language, but we can only speculate about his education. We know that the King's New School in Stratford-
upon-Avon was considered excellent. The school was
one of the English "grammar schools" established to
educate young men, primarily in Latin grammar and
literature. As in other schools of the time, students
began their studies at the age of four or five in the
attached "petty school," and there learned to read and
write in English, studying primarily the catechism from
the Book of Common Prayer. After two years in the petty
school, students entered the lower form (grade) of the
grammar school, where they began the serious study of
Latin grammar and Latin texts that would occupy most
of the remainder of their school days. (Several Latin
texts that Shakespeare used repeatedly in writing his
plays and poems were texts that schoolboys memorized
and recited.) Latin comedies were introduced early in
the lower form; in the upper form, which the boys
entered at age ten or eleven, students wrote their own
Latin orations and declamations, studied Latin historians and rhetoricians, and began the study of Greek using
the Greek New Testament.

Since the records of the Stratford "grammar school"
do not survive, we cannot prove that William Shakespeare attended the school; however, every indication
(his father's position as an alderman and bailiff of
Stratford, the playwright's own knowledge of the Latin
classics, scenes in the plays that recall grammar-school
experiences—for example, *The Merry Wives of Windsor*,
4.1) suggests that he did. We also lack generally accepted
documentation about Shakespeare's life after his
schooling ended and his professional life in London
began. His marriage in 1582 (at age eighteen) to Anne

Hathaway and the subsequent births of his daughter Susanna (1583) and the twins Judith and Hamnet (1585) are recorded, but how he supported himself and where he lived are not known. Nor do we know when and why he left Stratford for the London theatrical world, nor how he rose to be the important figure in that world that he had become by the early 1590s.

We do know that by 1592 he had achieved some prominence in London as both an actor and a playwright. In that year was published a book by the playwright Robert Greene attacking an actor who had the audacity to write blank-verse drama and who was "in his own conceit [i.e., opinion] the only Shake-scene in a country." Since Greene's attack includes a parody of a line from one of Shakespeare's early plays, there is little doubt that it is Shakespeare to whom he refers, a "Shake-scene" who had aroused Greene's fury by successfully competing with university-educated dramatists like Greene himself. It was in 1593 that Shakespeare became a published poet. In that year he published his long narrative poem *Venus and Adonis;* in 1594, he followed it with *The Rape of Lucrece.* Both poems were dedicated to the young earl of Southampton (Henry Wriothesley), who may have become Shakespeare's patron.

It seems no coincidence that Shakespeare wrote these narrative poems at a time when the theaters were closed because of the plague, a contagious epidemic disease that devastated the population of London. When the theaters reopened in 1594, Shakespeare apparently resumed his double career of actor and playwright and began his long (and seemingly profitable) service as an acting-company shareholder. Records for December of 1594 show him to be a leading member of the Lord Chamberlain's Men. It was this company of actors, later named the King's Men, for whom he would be a principal actor, dramatist, and shareholder for the rest of his career.

So far as we can tell, that career spanned about twenty years. In the 1590s, he wrote his plays on English history as well as several comedies and at least two tragedies (*Titus Andronicus* and *Romeo and Juliet*). These histories, comedies, and tragedies are the plays credited to him in 1598 in a work, *Palladis Tamia*, that in one chapter compares English writers with "Greek, Latin, and Italian Poets." There the author, Francis Meres, claims that Shakespeare is comparable to the Latin dramatists Seneca for tragedy and Plautus for comedy, and calls him "the most excellent in both kinds for the stage." He also names him "mellifluous and honey-tongued Shakespeare": "I say," writes Meres, "that the Muses would speak with Shakespeare's fine filed phrase, if they would speak English." Since Meres also mentions Shakespeare's "sugared sonnets among his private friends," it is assumed that many of Shakespeare's sonnets (not published until 1609) were also written in the 1590s.

In 1599, Shakespeare's company built a theater for themselves across the river from London, naming it the Globe. The plays that are considered by many to be Shakespeare's major tragedies (*Hamlet, Othello, King Lear,* and *Macbeth*) were written while the company was resident in this theater, as were such comedies as *Twelfth Night* and *Measure for Measure*. Many of Shakespeare's plays were performed at court (both for Queen Elizabeth I and, after her death in 1603, for King James I), some were presented at the Inns of Court (the residences of London's legal societies), and some were doubtless performed in other towns, at the universities, and at great houses when the King's Men went on tour; otherwise, his plays from 1599 to 1608 were, so far as we know, performed only at the Globe. Between 1608 and

1612, Shakespeare wrote several plays—among them *The Winter's Tale* and *The Tempest*—presumably for the company's new indoor Blackfriars theater, though the plays seem to have been performed also at the Globe and at court. Surviving documents describe a performance of *The Winter's Tale* in 1611 at the Globe, for example, and performances of *The Tempest* in 1611 and 1613 at the royal palace of Whitehall.

Shakespeare wrote very little after 1612, the year in which he probably wrote *King Henry VIII*. (It was at a performance of *Henry VIII* in 1613 that the Globe caught fire and burned to the ground.) Sometime between 1610 and 1613 he seems to have returned to live in Stratford-upon-Avon, where he owned a large house and considerable property, and where his wife and his two daughters and their husbands lived. (His son Hamnet had died in 1596.) During his professional years in London, Shakespeare had presumably derived income from the acting company's profits as well as from his own career as an actor, from the sale of his play manuscripts to the acting company, and, after 1599, from his shares as an owner of the Globe. It was presumably that income, carefully invested in land and other property, that made him the wealthy man that surviving documents show him to have become. It is also assumed that William Shakespeare's growing wealth and reputation played some part in inclining the crown, in 1596, to grant John Shakespeare, William's father, the coat of arms that he had so long sought. William Shakespeare died in Stratford on April 23, 1616 (according to the epitaph carved under his bust in Holy Trinity Church) and was buried on April 25. Seven years after his death, his collected plays were published as *Mr. William Shakespeares Comedies, Histories, & Tragedies* (the work now known as the First Folio).

The years in which Shakespeare wrote were among

the most exciting in English history. Intellectually, the discovery, translation, and printing of Greek and Roman classics were making available a set of works and worldviews that interacted complexly with Christian texts and beliefs. The result was a questioning, a vital intellectual ferment, that provided energy for the period's amazing dramatic and literary output and that fed directly into Shakespeare's plays. The Ghost in *Hamlet,* for example, is wonderfully complicated in part because he is a figure from Roman tragedy—the spirit of the dead returning to seek revenge—who at the same time inhabits a Christian hell (or purgatory); Hamlet's description of humankind reflects at one moment the Neoplatonic wonderment at mankind ("What a piece of work is a man!") and, at the next, the Christian disparagement of human sinners ("And yet, to me, what is this quintessence of dust?").

As intellectual horizons expanded, so also did geographical and cosmological horizons. New worlds— both North and South America—were explored, and in them were found human beings who lived and worshiped in ways radically different from those of Renaissance Europeans and Englishmen. The universe during these years also seemed to shift and expand. Copernicus had earlier theorized that the earth was not the center of the cosmos but revolved as a planet around the sun. Galileo's telescope, created in 1609, allowed scientists to see that Copernicus had been correct: the universe was not organized with the earth at the center, nor was it so nicely circumscribed as people had, until that time, thought. In terms of expanding horizons, the impact of these discoveries on people's beliefs—religious, scientific, and philosophical—cannot be overstated.

London, too, rapidly expanded and changed during the years (from the early 1590s to around 1610) that Shakespeare lived there. London—the center of England's government, its economy, its royal court, its overseas trade—was, during these years, becoming an exciting metropolis, drawing to it thousands of new citizens every year. Troubled by overcrowding, by poverty, by recurring epidemics of the plague, London was also a mecca for the wealthy and the aristocratic, and for those who sought advancement at court, or power in government or finance or trade. One hears in Shakespeare's plays the voices of London—the struggles for power, the fear of venereal disease, the language of buying and selling. One hears as well the voices of Stratford-upon-Avon—references to the nearby Forest of Arden, to sheep herding, to small-town gossip, to village fairs and markets. Part of the richness of Shakespeare's work is the influence felt there of the various worlds in which he lived: the world of metropolitan London, the world of small-town and rural England, the world of the theater, and the worlds of craftsmen and shepherds.

That Shakespeare inhabited such worlds we know from surviving London and Stratford documents, as well as from the evidence of the plays and poems themselves. From such records we can sketch the dramatist's life. We know from his works that he was a voracious reader. We know from legal and business documents that he was a multifaceted theater man who became a wealthy landowner. We know a bit about his family life and a fair amount about his legal and financial dealings. Most scholars today depend upon such evidence as they draw their picture of the world's greatest playwright. Such, however, has not always been the case. Until the late eighteenth century, the William Shakespeare who lived in most biographies was the creation of legend and tradition. This was the Shakespeare who was supposedly caught poaching deer at Charlecote, the estate of Sir Thomas Lucy close by

Stratford; this was the Shakespeare who fled from Sir Thomas's vengeance and made his way in London by taking care of horses outside a playhouse; this was the Shakespeare who reportedly could barely read, but whose natural gifts were extraordinary, whose father was a butcher who allowed his gifted son sometimes to help in the butcher shop, where William supposedly killed calves "in a high style," making a speech for the occasion. It was this legendary William Shakespeare whose Falstaff (in *1* and *2 Henry IV*) so pleased Queen Elizabeth that she demanded a play about Falstaff in love, and demanded that it be written in fourteen days (hence the existence of *The Merry Wives of Windsor*). It was this legendary Shakespeare who reached the top of his acting career in the roles of the Ghost in *Hamlet* and old Adam in *As You Like It*—and who died of a fever contracted by drinking too hard at "a merry meeting" with the poets Michael Drayton and Ben Jonson. This legendary Shakespeare is a rambunctious, undisciplined man, as attractively "wild" as his plays were seen by earlier generations to be. Unfortunately, there is no trace of evidence to support these wonderful stories.

Perhaps in response to the disreputable Shakespeare of legend—or perhaps in response to the fragmentary and, for some, all-too-ordinary Shakespeare documented by surviving records—some people since the mid-nineteenth century have argued that William Shakespeare could not have written the plays that bear his name. These persons have put forward some dozen names as more likely authors, among them Queen Elizabeth, Sir Francis Bacon, Edward de Vere (earl of Oxford), and Christopher Marlowe. Such attempts to find what for these people is a more believable author of the plays is a tribute to the regard in which the plays are held. Unfortunately for their claims, the documents that exist that provide evidence for the facts of Shakespeare's life tie him inextricably to the body of plays and poems that bear his name. Unlikely as it seems to those who want the works to have been written by an aristocrat, a university graduate, or an "important" person, the plays and poems seem clearly to have been produced by a man from Stratford-upon-Avon with a very good "grammar-school" education and a life of experience in London and in the world of the London theater. How this particular man produced the works that dominate the cultures of much of the world almost four hundred years after his death is one of life's mysteries—and one that will continue to tease our imaginations as we continue to delight in his plays and poems.

Shakespeare's Theater

The actors of Shakespeare's time are known to have performed plays in a great variety of locations. They played at court (that is, in the great halls of such royal residences as Whitehall, Hampton Court, and Greenwich); they played in halls at the universities of Oxford and Cambridge, and at the Inns of Court (the residences in London of the legal societies); and they also played in the private houses of great lords and civic officials. Sometimes acting companies went on tour from London into the provinces, often (but not only) when outbreaks of bubonic plague in the capital forced the closing of theaters to reduce the possibility of contagion in crowded audiences. In the provinces the actors usually staged their plays in churches (until around 1600) or in guildhalls. While surviving records show only a handful of occasions when actors played at inns while on tour, London inns were important playing places up until the 1590s.

The building of theaters in London had begun only shortly before Shakespeare wrote his first plays in the 1590s. These theaters were of two kinds: outdoor or public playhouses that could accommodate large numbers of playgoers, and indoor or private theaters for much smaller audiences. What is usually regarded as the first London outdoor public playhouse was called simply the Theatre. James Burbage—the father of Richard Burbage, who was perhaps the most famous actor in Shakespeare's company—built it in 1576 in an area north of the city of London called Shoreditch. Among the more famous of the other public playhouses that capitalized on the new fashion were the Curtain and the Fortune (both also built north of the city), the Rose, the Swan, the Globe, and the Hope (all located on the Bankside, a region just across the Thames south of the city of London). All these playhouses had to be built outside the jurisdiction of the city of London because many civic officials were hostile to the performance of drama and repeatedly petitioned the royal council to abolish it.

The theaters erected on the Bankside (a region under the authority of the Church of England, whose head was the monarch) shared the neighborhood with houses of prostitution and with the Paris Garden, where the blood sports of bearbaiting and bullbaiting were carried on. There may have been no clear distinction between playhouses and buildings for such sports, for we know that the Hope was used for both plays and baiting and that Philip Henslowe, owner of the Rose and, later, partner in the ownership of the Fortune, was also a partner in a monopoly on baiting. All these forms of entertainment were easily accessible to Londoners by boat across the Thames or over London Bridge.

Evidently Shakespeare's company prospered on the Bankside. They moved there in 1599. Threatened by difficulties in renewing the lease on the land where their first theater (the Theatre) had been built, Shakespeare's company took advantage of the Christmas holiday in 1598 to dismantle the Theatre and transport its timbers across the Thames to the Bankside, where, in 1599, these timbers were used in the building of the Globe. The weather in late December 1598 is recorded as having been especially harsh. It was so cold that the Thames was "nigh [nearly] frozen," and there was heavy snow. Perhaps the weather aided Shakespeare's company in eluding their landlord, the snow hiding their activity and the freezing of the Thames allowing them to slide the timbers across to the Bankside without paying tolls for repeated trips over London Bridge. Attractive as this narrative is, it remains just as likely that the heavy snow hampered transport of the timbers in wagons through the London streets to the river. It also must be remembered that the Thames was, according to report, only "nigh frozen" and therefore as impassable as it ever was. Whatever the precise circumstances of this fascinating event in English theater history, Shakespeare's company was able to begin playing at their new Globe theater on the Bankside in 1599. After the first Globe burned down in 1613 during the staging of Shakespeare's *Henry VIII* (its thatch roof was set alight by cannon fire called for by the performance), Shakespeare's company immediately rebuilt on the same location. The second Globe seems to have been a grander structure than its predecessor. It remained in use until the beginning of the English Civil War in 1642, when Parliament officially closed the theaters. Soon thereafter it was pulled down.

The public theaters of Shakespeare's time were very different buildings from our theaters today. First of all, they were open-air playhouses. As recent excavations of the Rose and the Globe confirm, some were polygonal or roughly circular in shape; the Fortune, however, was square. The most recent estimates of their size put the diameter of these buildings at 72 feet (the Rose) to 100 feet (the Globe), but we know that they held vast audiences of two or three thousand, who must have been squeezed together quite tightly. Some of these spectators paid extra to sit or stand in the two or three levels of roofed galleries that extended, on the upper levels, all the way around the theater and surrounded an open space. In this space were the stage and, perhaps, the tiring house (what we would call dressing rooms), as well as the so-called yard. In the yard stood the spectators who chose to pay less, the ones whom Hamlet contemptuously called "groundlings." For a roof they had only the sky, and so they were exposed to all kinds of weather. They stood on a floor that was sometimes made of mortar and sometimes of ash mixed with the shells of hazelnuts. The latter provided a porous and therefore dry footing for the crowd, and the shells may have been more comfortable to stand on because they were not as hard as mortar. Availability of shells may not have been a problem if hazelnuts were a favorite food for Shakespeare's audiences to munch on as they watched his plays. Archaeologists who are today unearthing the remains of theaters from this period have discovered quantities of these nutshells on theater sites.

Unlike the yard, the stage itself was covered by a roof. Its ceiling, called "the heavens," is thought to have been elaborately painted to depict the sun, moon, stars, and planets. Just how big the stage was remains hard to determine. We have a single sketch of part of the interior of the Swan. A Dutchman named Johannes de Witt visited this theater around 1596 and sent a sketch of it back to his friend, Arend van Buchel. Because van Buchel found de Witt's letter and sketch of interest, he copied both into a book. It is van Buchel's copy, adapted, it seems, to the shape and size of the page in his book, that survives. In this sketch, the stage appears to be a large rectangular platform that thrusts far out into the yard, perhaps even as far as the center of the circle formed by the surrounding galleries. This drawing, combined with the specifications for the size of the stage in the building contract for the Fortune, has led scholars to conjecture that the stage on which Shakespeare's plays were performed must have measured approximately 43 feet in width and 27 feet in depth, a vast acting area. But the digging up of a large part of the Rose by archaeologists has provided evidence of a quite different stage design. The Rose stage was a platform tapered at the corners and much shallower than what seems to be depicted in the van Buchel sketch. Indeed, its measurements seem to be about 37.5 feet across at its widest point and only 15.5 feet deep. Because the surviving indications of stage size and design differ from each other so much, it is possible that the stages in other theaters, like the Theatre, the Curtain, and the Globe (the outdoor playhouses where we know that Shakespeare's plays were performed), were different from those at both the Swan and the Rose.

After about 1608 Shakespeare's plays were staged not only at the Globe but also at an indoor or private playhouse in Blackfriars. This theater had been constructed in 1596 by James Burbage in an upper hall of a former Dominican priory or monastic house. Although Henry VIII had dissolved all English monasteries in the 1530s (shortly after he had founded the Church of England), the area remained under church, rather than hostile civic, control. The hall that Burbage had purchased and renovated was a large one in which Parliament had once met. In the private theater that he constructed, the stage, lit by candles, was built across the narrow end of the hall, with boxes flanking it. The rest of the hall offered seating room only. Because there was no provision for standing room, the largest audience it could hold was less than a thousand, or about a quarter of what the Globe could accommodate. Admission to Blackfriars was correspondingly more expensive. Instead of a penny to stand in the yard at the Globe, it cost a minimum of sixpence to get into Blackfriars. The best seats at the Globe (in the Lords' Room in the gallery above and behind the stage) cost sixpence; but the boxes flanking the stage at Blackfriars were half a crown, or five times sixpence. Some spectators who were particularly interested in displaying themselves paid even more to sit on stools on the Blackfriars stage.

Whether in the outdoor or indoor playhouses, the stages of Shakespeare's time were different from ours. They were not separated from the audience by the dropping of a curtain between acts and scenes. Therefore the playwrights of the time had to find other ways of signaling to the audience that one scene (to be imagined as occurring in one location at a given time) had ended and the next (to be imagined at perhaps a different location at a later time) had begun. The customary way used by Shakespeare and many of his contemporaries was to have everyone onstage exit at the end of one scene and have one or more different characters enter to begin the next. In a few cases, where characters remain onstage from one scene to another, the dialogue or stage action makes the change of location clear, and the characters are generally to be imagined as having moved from one place to another. For example, in *Romeo and Juliet*, Romeo and his friends remain onstage in Act 1 from scene 4 to scene 5, but they are represented as having moved between scenes from the street that leads to Capulet's house into Capulet's house itself. The new location is signaled in part by the appearance onstage of

Capulet's servingmen carrying napkins, something they would not take into the streets. Playwrights had to be quite resourceful in the use of hand properties, like the napkin, or in the use of dialogue to specify where the action was taking place in their plays because, in contrast to most of today's theaters, the playhouses of Shakespeare's time did not use movable scenery to dress the stage and make the setting precise. As another consequence of this difference, however, the playwrights of Shakespeare's time did not have to specify exactly where the action of their plays was set when they did not choose to do so, and much of the action of their plays is tied to no specific place.

Usually Shakespeare's stage is referred to as a "bare stage," to distinguish it from the stages of the last two or three centuries with their elaborate sets. But the stage in Shakespeare's time was not completely bare. Philip Henslowe, owner of the Rose, lists in his inventory of stage properties a rock, three tombs, and two mossy banks. Stage directions in plays of the time also call for such things as thrones (or "states"), banquets (presumably tables with plaster replicas of food on them), and beds and tombs to be pushed onto the stage. Thus the stage often held more than the actors.

The actors did not limit their performing to the stage alone. Occasionally they went beneath the stage, as the Ghost appears to do in the first act of *Hamlet*. From there they could emerge onto the stage through a trapdoor. They could retire behind the hangings across the back of the stage (or the front of the tiring house), as, for example, the actor playing Polonius does when he hides behind the arras. Sometimes the hangings could be drawn back during a performance to "discover" one or more actors behind them. When performance required that an actor appear "above," as when Juliet is imagined to stand at the window of her chamber in the famous and misnamed "balcony scene," then the actor probably climbed the stairs to the gallery over the back of the stage and temporarily shared it with some of the spectators. The stage was also provided with ropes and winches so that actors could descend from, and reascend to, the "heavens."

Perhaps the greatest difference between dramatic performances in Shakespeare's time and ours was that in Shakespeare's England the roles of women were played by boys. (Some of these boys grew up to take male roles in their maturity.) There were no women in the acting companies, only in the audience. It had not always been so in the history of the English stage. There are records of women on English stages in the thirteenth and fourteenth centuries, two hundred years before Shakespeare's plays were performed. After the accession of James I in 1603, the queen of England and her ladies took part in entertainments at court called masques, and with the reopening of the theaters in 1660 at the restoration of Charles II, women again took their place on the public stage.

The chief competitors for the companies of adult actors such as the one to which Shakespeare belonged and for which he wrote were companies of exclusively boy actors. The competition was most intense in the early 1600s. There were then two principal children's companies: the Children of Paul's (the choirboys from St. Paul's Cathedral, whose private playhouse was near the cathedral); and the Children of the Chapel Royal (the choirboys from the monarch's private chapel, who performed at the Blackfriars theater built by Burbage in 1596, which Shakespeare's company had been stopped from using by local residents who objected to crowds). In *Hamlet* Shakespeare writes of "an aerie [nest] of children, little eyases [hawks], that cry out on the top of question and are most tyrannically clapped for 't. These are now the fashion and . . . berattle the common stages [attack the public theaters]." In the long run, the adult actors prevailed. The Children of Paul's dissolved around 1606. By about 1608 the Children of the Chapel Royal had been forced to stop playing at the Blackfriars theater, which was then taken over by the King's Men, Shakespeare's own troupe.

Acting companies and theaters of Shakespeare's time were organized in different ways. For example, Philip Henslowe owned the Rose and leased it to companies of actors, who paid him from their takings. Henslowe would act as manager of these companies, initially paying playwrights for their plays and buying properties, recovering his outlay from the actors. Shakespeare's company, however, managed itself, with the principal actors, Shakespeare among them, having the status of "sharers" and the right to a share in the takings, as well as the responsibility for a part of the expenses. Five of the sharers themselves, Shakespeare among them, owned the Globe. As actor, as sharer in an acting company and in ownership of theaters, and as playwright, Shakespeare was about as involved in the theatrical industry as one could imagine. Although Shakespeare and his fellows prospered, their status under the law was conditional upon the protection of powerful patrons. "Common players"—those who did not have patrons or masters—were classed in the language of the law with "vagabonds and sturdy beggars." So the actors had to secure for themselves the official rank of servants of patrons. Among the patrons under whose protection Shakespeare's company worked were the lord chamberlain and, after the accession of King James in 1603, the king himself.

We are now perhaps on the verge of learning a great deal more about the theaters in which Shakespeare and his contemporaries performed—or at least of opening up new questions about them. Already about 70 percent of the Rose has been excavated, as has about 10 percent of the second Globe, the one built in 1614. It is to be hoped that soon more will be available for study. These are exciting times for students of Shakespeare's stage.

The Publication of Shakespeare's Plays

Eighteen of Shakespeare's plays found their way into print during the playwright's lifetime, but there is nothing to suggest that he took any interest in their publication. These eighteen appeared separately in editions called quartos. Their pages were not much larger than the one you are now reading, and these little books were sold unbound for a few pence. The earliest of the quartos that still survive were printed in 1594, the year that both *Titus Andronicus* and a version of the play now called *2 King Henry VI* became available. While almost every one of these early quartos displays on its title page the name of the acting company that performed the play, only about half provide the name of the playwright, Shakespeare. The first quarto edition to bear the name Shakespeare on its title page is *Love's Labor's Lost* of 1598. A few of these quartos were popular with the book-buying public of Shakespeare's lifetime; for example, quarto *Richard II* went through five editions between 1597 and 1615. But most of the quartos were far from best-sellers; *Love's Labor's Lost* (1598), for instance, was not reprinted in quarto until 1631. After Shakespeare's death, two more of his plays appeared in quarto format: *Othello* in 1622 and *The Two Noble Kinsmen,* coauthored with John Fletcher, in 1634.

In 1623, seven years after Shakespeare's death, *Mr. William Shakespeares Comedies, Histories, & Tragedies* was published. This printing offered readers in a single book thirty-six of the thirty-eight plays now thought to have been written by Shakespeare, including eighteen that had never been printed before. And it offered them in a style that was then reserved for serious literature and scholarship. The plays were arranged in double columns on pages nearly a foot high. This large page size is called "folio," as opposed to the smaller "quarto," and the 1623 volume is usually called the Shakespeare First Folio. It is reputed to have sold for the lordly price of a pound. (One copy at the Folger Library is marked fifteen shillings—that is, three-quarters of a pound.)

In a preface to the First Folio entitled "To the great Variety of Readers," two of Shakespeare's former fellow actors in the King's Men, John Heminge and Henry Condell, wrote that they themselves had collected their dead companion's plays. They suggested that they had seen his own papers: "we have scarce received from him a blot in his papers." The title page of the Folio declared that the plays within it had been printed "according to the True Original Copies." Comparing the Folio to the quartos, Heminge and Condell disparaged the quartos, advising their readers that "before you were abused with divers stolen and surreptitious copies, maimed, and deformed by the frauds and stealths of injurious impostors." Many Shakespeareans of the eighteenth and nineteenth centuries believed Heminge and Condell and regarded the Folio plays as superior to anything in the quartos.

Once we begin to examine the Folio plays in detail, it becomes less easy to take at face value the word of Heminge and Condell about the superiority of the Folio texts. For example, of the first nine plays in the Folio (one quarter of the entire collection), four were essentially reprinted from earlier quarto printings that Heminge and Condell had disparaged; and four have now been identified as printed from copies written in the hand of a professional scribe of the 1620s named Ralph Crane; the ninth, *The Comedy of Errors*, was apparently also printed from a manuscript, but one whose origin cannot be readily identified. Evidently then, eight of the first nine plays in the First Folio were not printed, in spite of what the Folio title page announces, "according to the True Original Copies," or Shakespeare's own papers, and the source of the ninth is unknown. Since today's editors have been forced to treat Heminge and Condell's pronouncements with skepticism, they must choose whether to base their own editions upon quartos or the Folio on grounds other than Heminge and Condell's story of where the quarto and Folio versions originated.

Editors have often fashioned their own narratives to explain what lies behind the quartos and Folio. They have said that Heminge and Condell meant to criticize only a few of the early quartos, the ones that offer much shorter and sometimes quite different, often garbled, versions of plays. Among the examples of these are the 1600 quarto of *Henry V* (the Folio offers a much fuller version) or the 1603 *Hamlet* quarto (in 1604 a different, much longer form of the play got into print as a quarto). Early in this century editors speculated that these questionable texts were produced when someone in the audience took notes from the plays' dialogue during performances and then employed "hack poets" to fill out the notes. The poor results were then sold to a publisher and presented in print as Shakespeare's plays. More recently this story has given way to another in which the shorter versions are said to be recreations from memory of Shakespeare's plays by actors who wanted to stage them in the provinces but lacked manuscript copies. Most of the quartos offer much better texts than these so-called bad quartos. Indeed, in most of the quartos we find texts that are at least equal to or better than what is printed in the Folio. Many of this century's Shakespeare enthusiasts have persuaded themselves that most of the quartos were set into type directly from Shakespeare's own papers, although there is nothing on which to base this conclusion except the desire for it to be true. Thus speculation continues about how the Shakespeare plays got to be printed. All that we have are the printed texts.

The book collector who was most successful in bringing together copies of the quartos and the First Folio was Henry Clay Folger, founder of the Folger Shakespeare Library in Washington, D.C. While it is estimated that there survive around the world only about 230 copies of the First Folio, Mr. Folger was able to acquire more than seventy-five copies, as well as a large number of fragments, for the library that bears his name. He also amassed a substantial number of quartos. For example, only fourteen copies of the First Quarto of *Love's Labor's Lost* are known to exist, and three are at the Folger Shakespeare Library. As a consequence of Mr. Folger's labors, twentieth-century scholars visiting the Folger Library have been able to learn a great deal about sixteenth- and seventeenth-century printing and, particularly, about the printing of Shakespeare's plays. And Mr. Folger did not stop at the First Folio, but collected many copies of later editions of Shakespeare, beginning with the Second Folio (1632), the Third (1663–64), and the Fourth (1685). Each of these later folios was based on its immediate predecessor and was edited anonymously. The first editor of Shakespeare whose name we know was Nicholas Rowe, whose first edition came out in 1709. Mr. Folger collected this edition and many, many more by Rowe's successors.

An Introduction to This Text

The Taming of the Shrew was first printed in the 1623 collection of Shakespeare's plays now known as the First Folio. However, in 1594 there was printed a play entitled *A Pleasant Conceited Historie, called The taming of a Shrew*. In many respects, the plot of *A Pleasant Conceited Historie* (1594) parallels in its major outline that of Shakespeare's *The Taming of the Shrew* (1623). But there are also a great many differences. *A Pleasant Conceited Historie* is only about half as long as *The Taming of the Shrew*. Many of its characters have quite different names; for example, Petruchio is called Ferando, and Tranio is called Valeria. Katherine has two sisters, and there is no character equivalent to Gremio. Furthermore, there is very little resemblance between the language of the two plays. It may be of interest to note that the Induction's plot involving the trick being played on the beggar Sly is continued in *A Pleasant Conceited Historie* until the end of the play, when Sly, who has fallen asleep during the play-within-the-play, is returned to the alehouse where we first found him. Because of the large and important differences between the two plays, this edition of *The Taming of the Shrew* almost entirely ignores *A Pleasant Conceited Historie*.

Instead, the present edition is based directly upon the First Folio version.* For the convenience of the reader, we have modernized the punctuation and the spelling of the Folio. Sometimes we go so far as to modernize certain old forms of words; for example, when *a* means

---

*We have also consulted the computerized text of the First Folio provided by the Text Archive of the Oxford University Computing Centre, to which we are grateful.

"he," we change it to *he;* we change *mo* to *more* and *ye* to *you.* But it is not our practice in editing any of the plays to modernize words that sound distinctly different from modern forms. For example, when the early printed texts read *sith* or *apricocks* or *porpentine,* we have not modernized to *since, apricots, porcupine.* When the forms *an, and,* or *and if* appear instead of the modern form *if,* we have reduced *and* to *an* but have not changed any of these forms to their modern equivalent, *if.* We also modernize and, where necessary, correct passages in foreign languages, unless an error in the early printed text can be reasonably explained as a joke. Whenever we change the wording of the First Folio or add anything to its stage directions, we mark the change by enclosing it in superior half-brackets (⌐⌐). We want our readers to be immediately aware when we have intervened. (Only when we correct an obvious typographical error in the First Folio does the change not get marked.) Whenever we change the First Folio's wording or its punctuation so that meaning changes, we list the change in the textual notes at the back of the book, even if all we have done is fix an obvious error.

We regularize a number of the proper names, as is the usual practice in editions of the play. For example, the Folio sometimes calls Katherine "Katherina." Except where the verse requires "Katherina," we print Katherine throughout this text.

This edition differs from many earlier ones in its efforts to aid the reader in imagining the play as a performance rather than as a series of actual events. Thus stage directions are written with reference to the stage. Whenever it is reasonably certain, in our view, that a speech is accompanied by a particular action, we provide a stage direction describing the action. (Occasional exceptions to this rule occur when the action is so obvious that to add a stage direction would insult the reader.) Stage directions for the entrance of characters in mid-scene are, with rare exceptions, placed so that they immediately precede the characters' participation in the scene, even though these entrances may appear somewhat earlier in the early printed texts. Whenever we move a stage direction, we record this change in the textual notes. Latin stage directions (e.g., *Exeunt*) are translated into English (e.g., *They exit*).

We expand the often severely abbreviated forms of names used as speech headings in early printed texts into the full names of the characters. We also regularize the speakers' names in speech headings, using only a single designation for each character, even though the early printed texts sometimes use a variety of designations. Variations in the speech headings of the early printed texts are recorded in the textual notes.

In the present edition, as well, we mark with a dash any change of address within a speech, unless a stage direction intervenes. When the *-ed* ending of a word is to be pronounced, we mark it with an accent. Like editors for the last two centuries, we print metrically linked lines in the following way:

> PETRUCHIO
> I am content.
> KATHERINE   Are you content to stay?

However, when there are a number of short verse-lines that can be linked in more than one way, we do not, with rare exceptions, indent any of them.

The Explanatory Notes

The notes that appear on the pages facing the text are designed to provide readers with the help that they may need to enjoy the play. Whenever the meaning of a word in the text is not readily accessible in a good contemporary dictionary, we offer the meaning in a note. Sometimes we provide a note even when the relevant meaning is to be found in the dictionary but when the word has acquired since Shakespeare's time other potentially confusing meanings. In our notes, we try to offer modern synonyms for Shakespeare's words. We also try to indicate to the reader the connection between the word in the play and the modern synonym. For example, Shakespeare sometimes uses the word *head* to mean "source," but, for modern readers, there may be no connection evident between these two words. We provide the connection by explaining Shakespeare's usage as follows: "**head:** fountainhead, source." On some occasions, a whole phrase or clause needs explanation. Then we rephrase in our own words the difficult passage, and add at the end synonyms for individual words in the passage. When scholars have been unable to determine the meaning of a word or phrase, we acknowledge the uncertainty.

THE
TAMING
OF THE
SHREW

Characters in the Play

CHRISTOPHER SLY, a beggar ⎫
Hostess of an alehouse   ⎪
A Lord   ⎪
Huntsmen of the Lord   ⎬ *characters in*
Page (disguised as a lady)   ⎪ *the Induction*
Players   ⎪
Servingmen   ⎪
Messenger   ⎭

BAPTISTA MINOLA, father to Katherine and Bianca
KATHERINE, his elder daughter
BIANCA, his younger daughter

PETRUCHIO, suitor to Katherine

GREMIO   ⎫
HORTENSIO (later disguised as   ⎪
    the teacher Litio)   ⎬ *suitors to Bianca*
LUCENTIO (later disguised as   ⎪
    the teacher Cambio) ⎭

VINCENTIO, Lucentio's father

TRANIO (later impersonating   ⎫
    Lucentio)   ⎬ *servants to Lucentio*
BIONDELLO   ⎭
A Merchant (later disguised as Vincentio)

3

GRUMIO
CURTIS
NATHANIEL
PHILLIP   } *servants to Petruchio*
JOSEPH
NICHOLAS
PETER

Widow

Tailor
Haberdasher
Officer

Servants to Baptista and Petruchio

THE
TAMING
OF THE
SHREW

INDUCTION

Ind.1 Christopher Sly, a drunken beggar, is driven out of an alehouse by its hostess. A great lord, returning from the hunt, finds Sly in a drunken sleep and decides to play an elaborate trick on him. The lord orders his servants to place Sly in a luxurious bedroom and, when the beggar awakes, to tell him he is a great lord who has long been out of his mind. A troupe of traveling actors present themselves to the lord, who, by way of further elaborating his trick, instructs them to stage a play for Sly.

----

1. **feeze you:** fix you, do for you
2. **stocks:** a heavy timber frame with holes for the ankles used to punish disturbers of the peace
4. **chronicles:** histories, such as Holinshed's *Chronicles* (1577 and 1587), often used by Shakespeare
4–5. **Richard Conqueror:** i.e., William the Conqueror
5. **paucas pallabris:** i.e., *pocas palabras*, Spanish for "few words," i.e., enough
6. **Sessa:** perhaps French *cessez* or Spanish *cesa*, both meaning "stop" or "be silent"
9. **denier:** small copper coin of little value; **Saint Jeronimy:** St. Jerome (Some scholars think **Jeronimy** a reference to Hieronimo, the hero of Kyd's play *The Spanish Tragedy*.)
12. **headborough:** constable
13. **Third . . . borough:** "Thirdborough" was another term for constable.
15. **kindly:** i.e., welcome
15 SD. **Wind:** blow

(continued)

⌈INDUCTION⌉

Scene 1
Enter Beggar (Christopher Sly) and Hostess.

SLY   I'll feeze you, in faith.

HOSTESS   A pair of stocks, you rogue!

SLY   You're a baggage! The Slys are no rogues. Look
in the chronicles. We came in with Richard Conqueror. Therefore, *paucas pallabris*, let the world   5
slide. Sessa!

HOSTESS   You will not pay for the glasses you have
burst?

SLY   No, not a denier. Go, by ⌈Saint⌉ Jeronimy! Go to
thy cold bed and warm thee.   ⌈*He lies down.*⌉   10

HOSTESS   I know my remedy. I must go fetch the
headborough.   ⌈*She exits.*⌉

SLY   Third, or fourth, or fifth borough, I'll answer him
by law. I'll not budge an inch, boy. Let him come,
and kindly.   *Falls asleep.*   15

Wind horns ⌈*within.*⌉ *Enter a Lord from hunting, with*
his train.

LORD
Huntsman, I charge thee tender well my hounds.
⌈Breathe⌉ Merriman (the poor cur is embossed)
And couple Clowder with the deep-mouthed brach.
Saw'st thou not, boy, how Silver made it good
At the hedge corner, in the coldest fault?   20
I would not lose the dog for twenty pound!

7

16. **tender well:** take good care of
17. **Breathe Merriman:** let Merriman get his breath back; **embossed:** exhausted
19. **made it good:** i.e., picked up the scent
20. **in . . . fault:** i.e., when the scent was lost
23. **it:** i.e., the scent; **at the merest loss:** i.e., when the scent was absolutely lost
36. **thine image:** i.e., sleep, which looks like death
37. **practice:** play a trick on
42. **brave:** splendidly dressed
44. **cannot choose:** i.e., will have no other choice

FIRST HUNTSMAN
  Why, Bellman is as good as he, my lord.
  He cried upon it at the merest loss,
  And twice today picked out the dullest scent.
  Trust me, I take him for the better dog.   25
LORD
  Thou art a fool. If Echo were as fleet,
  I would esteem him worth a dozen such.
  But sup them well, and look unto them all.
  Tomorrow I intend to hunt again.
FIRST HUNTSMAN   I will, my lord.   30
                           ⌜*First Huntsman exits.*⌝
LORD, ⌜*noticing Sly*⌝
  What's here? One dead, or drunk? See doth he
    breathe.
SECOND HUNTSMAN
  He breathes, my lord. Were he not warmed with ale,
  This were a bed but cold to sleep so soundly.
LORD
  O monstrous beast, how like a swine he lies!   35
  Grim death, how foul and loathsome is thine image!
  Sirs, I will practice on this drunken man.
  What think you, if he were conveyed to bed,
  Wrapped in sweet clothes, rings put upon his
    fingers,   40
  A most delicious banquet by his bed,
  And brave attendants near him when he wakes,
  Would not the beggar then forget himself?
⌜THIRD⌝ HUNTSMAN
  Believe me, lord, I think he cannot choose.
SECOND HUNTSMAN
  It would seem strange unto him when he waked.   45
LORD
  Even as a flatt'ring dream or worthless fancy.
  Then take him up, and manage well the jest.

54. **straight:** immediately
55. **reverence:** bow
59. **diaper:** small towel
67. **when . . . is:** i.e., when he says he is now mad
69. **kindly:** (1) naturally—with no sign that you are feigning; (2) in a friendly way
70. **passing:** surpassingly
71. **husbanded with modesty:** conducted with restraint
73. **As:** i.e., so that
76. **office:** assigned part; **he:** i.e., Sly
77. **Sirrah:** a term of address to a social inferior

A ewer and basin. (IND.1.57, 59)
From Bartolomeo Scappi, *Opera . . .* (1605).

Carry him gently to my fairest chamber,
And hang it round with all my wanton pictures;
Balm his foul head in warm distillèd waters,   50
And burn sweet wood to make the lodging sweet;
Procure me music ready when he wakes
To make a dulcet and a heavenly sound.
And if he chance to speak, be ready straight
And, with a low, submissive reverence,   55
Say "What is it your Honor will command?"
Let one attend him with a silver basin
Full of rosewater and bestrewed with flowers,
Another bear the ewer, the third a diaper,
And say "Will 't please your Lordship cool your   60
    hands?"
Someone be ready with a costly suit,
And ask him what apparel he will wear.
Another tell him of his hounds and horse,
And that his lady mourns at his disease.   65
Persuade him that he hath been lunatic,
And when he says he is, say that he dreams,
For he is nothing but a mighty lord.
This do, and do it kindly, gentle sirs.
It will be pastime passing excellent   70
If it be husbanded with modesty.

⌈THIRD⌉ HUNTSMAN
My lord, I warrant you we will play our part
As he shall think by our true diligence
He is no less than what we say he is.

LORD
Take him up gently, and to bed with him,   75
And each one to his office when he wakes.
                            ⌈*Sly is carried out.*⌉
                         Sound trumpets ⌈*within.*⌉
Sirrah, go see what trumpet 'tis that sounds.
                            ⌈*Servingman exits.*⌉

11

78. **Belike:** probably; **means:** intends
81. **An 't:** if it; **players:** actors
87. **So please:** if it please; **duty:** respect
91. **sure:** certainly
92. **aptly fitted:** well cast
93. **Soto:** The earliest surviving play with a character named Soto is John Fletcher's *Women Pleased* (1619). Since only a fraction of the drama of Shakespeare's time survives, it is likely that the reference here is to a lost play.
95. **in happy time:** i.e., at just the right moment
96. **The rather for:** i.e., especially because
97. **cunning:** skill
99. **doubtful of your modesties:** i.e., suspicious about how well you can control yourselves
100. **over-eying of:** observing
102. **merry passion:** i.e., laughter

Belike some noble gentleman that means
(Traveling some journey) to repose him here.

Enter Servingman.

How now? Who is it?   80
SERVINGMAN   An 't please your Honor, players
That offer service to your Lordship.
LORD
Bid them come near.

Enter Players.

                  Now, fellows, you are welcome.
PLAYERS   We thank your Honor.   85
LORD
Do you intend to stay with me tonight?
⌜FIRST PLAYER⌝
So please your Lordship to accept our duty.
LORD
With all my heart. This fellow I remember
Since once he played a farmer's eldest son.—
'Twas where you wooed the gentlewoman so well.   90
I have forgot your name, but sure that part
Was aptly fitted and naturally performed.
⌜SECOND PLAYER⌝
I think 'twas Soto that your Honor means.
LORD
'Tis very true. Thou didst it excellent.
Well, you are come to me in happy time,   95
The rather for I have some sport in hand
Wherein your cunning can assist me much.
There is a lord will hear you play tonight;
But I am doubtful of your modesties,
Lest, over-eying of his odd behavior   100
(For yet his Honor never heard a play),
You break into some merry passion,
And so offend him. For I tell you, sirs,
If you should smile, he grows impatient.

13

106. **veriest antic:** the most peculiar person
107. **buttery:** storeroom for food and drink
109. **want:** lack; **affords:** can provide
110. **Bartholomew:** pronounced "Bartelmy"
111. **in all suits:** in every way
113–14. **him . . . him . . . him:** i.e., the page
114. **as he will:** i.e., if he wishes to
115. **He bear:** i.e., he should conduct
117. **accomplishèd:** performed
119. **tongue:** voice
124. **with . . . bosom:** with his (the page's) head lowered onto Sly's breast
125. **him:** i.e., the page; **as being:** i.e., as if he were
127. **esteemed him:** i.e., thought himself to be
131. **shift:** trick
132. **napkin:** handkerchief; **close conveyed:** secretly carried
133. **Shall . . . eye:** despite his inability to cry, will force his eyes to water
135. **Anon:** soon
136. **usurp:** take on

⌐FIRST PLAYER⌐
    Fear not, my lord, we can contain ourselves   105
    Were he the veriest antic in the world.
LORD, ⌐*to a Servingman*⌐
    Go, sirrah, take them to the buttery
    And give them friendly welcome every one.
    Let them want nothing that my house affords.
                        One exits with the Players.
    Sirrah, go you to Bartholomew, my page,   110
    And see him dressed in all suits like a lady.
    That done, conduct him to the drunkard's chamber,
    And call him "Madam," do him obeisance.
    Tell him from me, as he will win my love,
    He bear himself with honorable action,   115
    Such as he hath observed in noble ladies
    Unto their lords, by them accomplishèd.
    Such duty to the drunkard let him do
    With soft low tongue and lowly courtesy,
    And say "What is 't your Honor will command,   120
    Wherein your lady and your humble wife
    May show her duty and make known her love?"
    And then with kind embracements, tempting kisses,
    And with declining head into his bosom,
    Bid him shed tears, as being overjoyed   125
    To see her noble lord restored to health,
    Who, for this seven years, hath esteemed him
    No better than a poor and loathsome beggar.
    And if the boy have not a woman's gift
    To rain a shower of commanded tears,   130
    An onion will do well for such a shift,
    Which (in a napkin being close conveyed)
    Shall in despite enforce a watery eye.
    See this dispatched with all the haste thou canst.
    Anon I'll give thee more instructions.   135
                        A Servingman exits.
    I know the boy will well usurp the grace,

139. **stay:** stop, keep
141. **do homage:** show respect
142. **Haply:** perhaps
143. **over-merry spleen:** excess of laughter (The spleen was thought to be the seat of laughter, as well as of other strong emotions.)

Ind.2 The newly awakened Sly is offered delicacies and fine clothes. When he demands his usual ale and beef, the lord and servants tell him that he is suffering from delusions. After they inform him that he has a beautiful wife, he asks to see her. The lord's page, who impersonates the wife, persuades Sly to watch the play that is about to begin.

———————

1. **small:** thin, weak, and therefore cheap
2. **sack:** costly dry Spanish wine, such as sherry
3. **conserves:** candied fruit
6. **An if:** i.e., if
7. **conserves of beef:** salted beef
9. **doublets:** i.e., jackets
13. **idle humor:** groundless fantasy

Voice, gait, and action of a gentlewoman.
I long to hear him call the drunkard "husband"!
And how my men will stay themselves from
    laughter   140
When they do homage to this simple peasant,
I'll in to counsel them. Haply my presence
May well abate the over-merry spleen
Which otherwise would grow into extremes.
                                ⌜*They exit.*⌝

⌜Scene 2⌝
Enter aloft ⌜*Christopher Sly,*⌝ *the drunkard, with
Attendants, some with apparel, basin and ewer, and
other appurtenances, and Lord* ⌜*dressed as an Attendant.*⌝

SLY   For God's sake, a pot of small ale.
FIRST SERVINGMAN
    Will 't please your Lord drink a cup of sack?
SECOND SERVINGMAN
    Will 't please your Honor taste of these conserves?
THIRD SERVINGMAN
    What raiment will your Honor wear today?
SLY   I am Christophero Sly! Call not me "Honor" nor   5
    "Lordship." I ne'er drank sack in my life. An if you
    give me any conserves, give me conserves of beef.
    Ne'er ask me what raiment I'll wear, for I have no
    more doublets than backs, no more stockings than
    legs, nor no more shoes than feet, nay sometime   10
    more feet than shoes, or such shoes as my toes look
    through the over-leather.
LORD, ⌜*as* ATTENDANT⌝
    Heaven cease this idle humor in your Honor!
    O, that a mighty man of such descent,
    Of such possessions, and so high esteem   15
    Should be infusèd with so foul a spirit!

17

18. **Burton Heath:** perhaps Barton-on-the-Heath, a village about a dozen miles from Shakespeare's native Stratford

19. **cardmaker:** maker of cards used to comb wool

20. **bearherd:** keeper of a tame, performing bear (See page 26.)

21. **alewife:** woman alehousekeeper

21–22. **Wincot:** another village near Stratford

23. **on the score:** on account (Charges for drink were cut or scored on a stick or tally.); **sheer ale:** ale alone; or, perhaps, "small ale"; **score me up:** chalk me up

25. **bestraught:** distracted

30. **bethink thee:** think

31. **ancient:** former

34. **office:** assignment

35. **Apollo:** here, patron god of music (See page 80.)

39. **Semiramis:** queen of Assyria, noted for her sexual escapades

40. **bestrew:** cover with flowers or rushes

41. **trapped:** dressed in trappings

43. **hawking:** hunting for birds with trained hawks

45–46. **Thy hounds . . . earth:** i.e., the sound of the hounds' barking will strike the sky and then return to echo from the earth **welkin:** the sky

47. **course:** hunt hares with greyhounds

48. **breathèd stags:** stags with good wind or endurance; **roe:** small deer

SLY   What, would you make me mad? Am not I Chris-
     topher Sly, old Sly's son of Burton Heath, by birth a
     peddler, by education a cardmaker, by transmuta-
     tion a bearherd, and now by present profession a   20
     tinker? Ask Marian Hacket, the fat alewife of Win-
     cot, if she know me not! If she say I am not fourteen
     pence on the score for sheer ale, score me up for the
     lying'st knave in Christendom. What, I am not
     bestraught! Here's—   25
THIRD SERVINGMAN
     O, this it is that makes your lady mourn.
SECOND SERVINGMAN
     O, this is it that makes your servants droop.
LORD, ⌈as ATTENDANT⌉
     Hence comes it that your kindred shuns your house,
     As beaten hence by your strange lunacy.
     O noble lord, bethink thee of thy birth,   30
     Call home thy ancient thoughts from banishment,
     And banish hence these abject lowly dreams.
     Look how thy servants do attend on thee,
     Each in his office ready at thy beck.
     Wilt thou have music? Hark, Apollo plays,   *Music.*   35
     And twenty cagèd nightingales do sing.
     Or wilt thou sleep? We'll have thee to a couch
     Softer and sweeter than the lustful bed
     On purpose trimmed up for Semiramis.
     Say thou wilt walk, we will bestrew the ground.   40
     Or wilt thou ride? Thy horses shall be trapped,
     Their harness studded all with gold and pearl.
     Dost thou love hawking? Thou hast hawks will soar
     Above the morning lark. Or wilt thou hunt?
     Thy hounds shall make the welkin answer them   45
     And fetch shrill echoes from the hollow earth.
FIRST SERVINGMAN
     Say thou wilt course. Thy greyhounds are as swift
     As breathèd stags, ay, fleeter than the roe.

19

49. pictures: These are presumably the "wanton pictures" mentioned by the lord in Induction 1. Now, in lines 49–60, are described pictures of seductions and rapes based on stories told in Ovid's *Metamorphoses:* the story of Venus and Adonis, of Jove and Io, of Apollo and Daphne.

50. Adonis: a mortal loved by Cytherea (i.e., Venus)

51. sedges: marsh grass

52. wanton: move playfully and lovingly

54. Io: a maiden raped by Jove and transformed into a heifer

55. beguilèd and surprised: tricked and captured

56. As lively . . . done: i.e., painted as vividly as if it were the actual deed

57. Daphne: a maiden desired and pursued by Apollo (She escaped when she was transformed into a laurel tree; see page 24.)

60. workmanly: expertly

65. envious: malicious; **o'errun:** overran

67. yet: even now

71. savors: odors

74. our: Sly now uses the royal "we."

75. smallest: thinnest, weakest, cheapest

77. wit: mind

SECOND SERVINGMAN
  Dost thou love pictures? We will fetch thee straight
  Adonis painted by a running brook,   50
  And Cytherea all in sedges hid,
  Which seem to move and wanton with her breath,
  Even as the waving sedges play with wind.
LORD, ⌜as ATTENDANT⌝
  We'll show thee Io as she was a maid
  And how she was beguilèd and surprised,   55
  As lively painted as the deed was done.
THIRD SERVINGMAN
  Or Daphne roaming through a thorny wood,
  Scratching her legs that one shall swear she bleeds,
  And at that sight shall sad Apollo weep,
  So workmanly the blood and tears are drawn.   60
LORD, ⌜as ATTENDANT⌝
  Thou art a lord, and nothing but a lord;
  Thou hast a lady far more beautiful
  Than any woman in this waning age.
FIRST SERVINGMAN
  And till the tears that she hath shed for thee
  Like envious floods o'errun her lovely face,   65
  She was the fairest creature in the world—
  And yet she is inferior to none.
SLY
  Am I a lord, and have I such a lady?
  Or do I dream? Or have I dreamed till now?
  I do not sleep: I see, I hear, I speak,   70
  I smell sweet savors, and I feel soft things.
  Upon my life, I am a lord indeed
  And not a tinker, nor Christopher Sly.
  Well, bring our lady hither to our sight,
  And once again a pot o' the smallest ale.   75
SECOND SERVINGMAN
  Will 't please your Mightiness to wash your hands?
  O, how we joy to see your wit restored!

78. **knew but:** only knew
79. **These:** i.e., these last
81. **fay:** faith
82. **of:** in
83. **idle:** silly
86. **house:** alehouse
87. **present . . . leet:** accuse her before the court of the lord of the manor
88–89. **stone jugs . . . quarts:** Customers preferred sealed quarts, which bore official stamps (seals) guaranteeing the quantity they contained, rather than stone jars that could hold indeterminate quantities.
91. **Ay:** yes
93. **reckoned up:** listed
94. **Greete:** a hamlet in Gloucestershire, near Stratford (The Folio reading, "Greece," seems to be a misreading.)
98. **amends:** recovery
102. **Marry:** i.e., indeed (originally an oath on the name of the Virgin Mary); **cheer:** food and drink
106. **goodman:** the form in which a lower-class wife addressed her husband

O, that once more you knew but what you are!
These fifteen years you have been in a dream,
Or, when you waked, so waked as if you slept.   80

SLY
These fifteen years! By my fay, a goodly nap.
But did I never speak of all that time?

FIRST SERVINGMAN
Oh, yes, my lord, but very idle words.
For though you lay here in this goodly chamber,
Yet would you say you were beaten out of door,   85
And rail upon the hostess of the house,
And say you would present her at the leet
Because she brought stone jugs and no sealed
    quarts.
Sometimes you would call out for Cicely Hacket.   90

SLY   Ay, the woman's maid of the house.

THIRD SERVINGMAN
Why, sir, you know no house, nor no such maid,
Nor no such men as you have reckoned up,
As Stephen Sly and old John Naps of ⌜Greete,⌝
And Peter Turph and Henry Pimpernell,   95
And twenty more such names and men as these,
Which never were, nor no man ever saw.

SLY   Now, Lord be thanked for my good amends!

ALL   Amen.

SLY   I thank thee. Thou shalt not lose by it.   100

Enter ⌜*Page as*⌝ *Lady, with Attendants.*

⌜PAGE, *as*⌝ LADY   How fares my noble lord?

SLY   Marry, I fare well, for here is cheer enough.
    Where is my wife?

⌜PAGE, *as*⌝ LADY
Here, noble lord. What is thy will with her?

SLY
Are you my wife, and will not call me "husband"?   105
My men should call me "lord." I am your goodman.

23

114. **above:** more than

116. **abandoned:** banished

123. **In peril . . . malady:** because of the danger that you will again fall ill

125. **stands:** will serve (There is a bawdy pun on **stands** when it is repeated in the next line.)

126. **tarry:** wait

130. **players:** actors; **amendment:** recovery

132. **hold . . . meet:** regard it to be most suitable

Apollo and Daphne. (IND.2.57, 59)
From Natale Conti, *Mythologiae* . . . (1616).

⌐PAGE, *as*⌐ LADY
  My husband and my lord, my lord and husband,
  I am your wife in all obedience.
SLY
  I know it well.—What must I call her?
LORD, ⌐*as* ATTENDANT⌐   "Madam."   110
SLY   "Alice Madam," or "Joan Madam"?
LORD
  "Madam," and nothing else. So lords call ladies.
SLY
  Madam wife, they say that I have dreamed
  And slept above some fifteen year or more.
⌐PAGE, *as*⌐ LADY
  Ay, and the time seems thirty unto me,   115
  Being all this time abandoned from your bed.
SLY
  'Tis much.—Servants, leave me and her alone.—
  Madam, undress you, and come now to bed.
⌐PAGE, *as*⌐ LADY
  Thrice noble lord, let me entreat of you
  To pardon me yet for a night or two;   120
  Or if not so, until the sun be set.
  For your physicians have expressly charged,
  In peril to incur your former malady,
  That I should yet absent me from your bed.
  I hope this reason stands for my excuse.   125
SLY   Ay, it stands so that I may hardly tarry so long; but
  I would be loath to fall into my dreams again. I will
  therefore tarry in despite of the flesh and the
  blood.

                    Enter a Messenger.

MESSENGER
  Your Honor's players, hearing your amendment,   130
  Are come to play a pleasant comedy,
  For so your doctors hold it very meet,

138. **bars:** prevents

140. **comonty:** i.e., comedy; **gambold:** i.e., frolic, merrymaking

143. **household stuff:** goods, utensils, dishes, etc. belonging to a household

144. **history:** i.e., story

A bearherd. (IND.2.20)
From Jacobus a. Bruck, *Emblemata moralia* . . . (1615).

Seeing too much sadness hath congealed your
  blood,
And melancholy is the nurse of frenzy.   135
Therefore they thought it good you hear a play
And frame your mind to mirth and merriment,
Which bars a thousand harms and lengthens life.

SLY Marry, I will. Let them play it. ⌜*Messenger exits.*⌝
    Is not a comonty a Christmas gambold or a tum-   140
    bling trick?

⌜PAGE, *as*⌝ LADY
No, my good lord, it is more pleasing stuff.

SLY What, household stuff?

⌜PAGE, *as*⌝ LADY   It is a kind of history.

SLY Well, we'll see 't. Come, madam wife, sit by my   145
    side, and let the world slip. We shall ne'er be
    younger.
                              ⌜*They sit.*⌝

27

THE
TAMING
OF THE
SHREW

ACT 1

1.1 Lucentio has come with his servant Tranio to Padua to study philosophy. They witness an encounter between Baptista and his daughters, in which Baptista announces that Bianca cannot marry until the elder and bad-tempered Katherine does. Bianca's suitors decide to search for a husband for Katherine. Meanwhile Lucentio has fallen in love with Bianca and decides to have Tranio impersonate him so that Lucentio, in the disguise of a schoolmaster, can secretly woo Bianca. The two men exchange clothes.

---

0 SD. **Flourish:** a fanfare of trumpets

1. **for:** because of

2. **nursery of arts:** Padua was famous for its university. **arts:** i.e., the liberal arts

3. **am arrived for:** i.e., have arrived in

5. **leave:** permission

7. **well approved:** found perfectly reliable

8. **breathe:** pause, rest, remain; **haply:** perhaps; **institute:** i.e., begin

9. **ingenious:** highly intellectual

10. **grave:** worthy and serious

11. **my father first:** i.e., my father before me

12. **of great traffic:** i.e., trading extensively

13. **come of:** descended from

14–16. **Vincentio's son . . . deeds:** i.e., it will be fitting for me, Vincentio's son, to fulfill all expectations by adorning his good fortune with good deeds

17. **the:** i.e., this

19–20. **Will I apply . . . achieved:** i.e., I will devote myself to that part of philosophy that deals with the happiness achieved through virtue

\ulcornerACT 1\urcorner

\ulcornerScene 1\urcorner

Flourish. Enter Lucentio, and his man Tranio.

LUCENTIO
Tranio, since for the great desire I had
To see fair Padua, nursery of arts,
I am arrived for fruitful Lombardy,
The pleasant garden of great Italy,
And by my father's love and leave am armed   5
With his goodwill and thy good company.
My trusty servant well approved in all,
Here let us breathe and haply institute
A course of learning and ingenious studies.
Pisa, renownèd for grave citizens,   10
Gave me my being, and my father first,
A merchant of great traffic through the world,
⌜Vincentio,⌝ come of the Bentivolii.
Vincentio's son, brought up in Florence,
It shall become to serve all hopes conceived   15
To deck his fortune with his virtuous deeds.
And therefore, Tranio, for the time I study
Virtue, and that part of philosophy
Will I apply that treats of happiness
By virtue specially to be achieved.   20
Tell me thy mind, for I have Pisa left
And am to Padua come, as he that leaves

31

23. **plash:** pool, puddle
25. **Mi perdonato:** excuse me, pardon me
26. **affected:** i.e., of the same feeling
30. **discipline:** i.e., philosophy
31. **stoics:** persons who put aside all pleasures, refusing to give in to emotion and desire (There is a play here on the word **stocks,** i.e., unfeeling people.)
32. **devote:** devoted; **Aristotle's checks:** the self-restraint which the Greek philosopher Aristotle (384–322 B.C.) advocated
33. **As:** i.e., so that; **Ovid:** Roman love poet (In his *Art of Love,* Ovid names himself the Professor of Love.); **abjured:** renounced
34. **Balk logic:** avoid the study of logic; or, chop logic, bandy words
35. **practice . . . talk:** i.e., instead of studying rhetoric in the university, practice rhetoric by talking with friends
36. **Music . . . quicken you:** i.e., use music and poetry to enliven you
38. **your stomach serves you:** you have an appetite for them
40. **affect:** like
41. **Gramercies:** thanks
42. **Biondello:** an (absent) servant of Lucentio's
43. **put us in readiness:** prepare ourselves
45 SD. **pantaloon:** ridiculous old man, a stock character in Italian comedy of the period (See page 34.)
47. **show:** entertainment, spectacle

A shallow plash to plunge him in the deep
And with satiety seeks to quench his thirst.
TRANIO
⌐Mi perdonato,¬ gentle master mine.   25
I am in all affected as yourself,
Glad that you thus continue your resolve
To suck the sweets of sweet philosophy.
Only, good master, while we do admire
This virtue and this moral discipline,   30
Let's be no stoics nor no stocks, I pray,
Or so devote to Aristotle's checks
As Ovid be an outcast quite abjured.
Balk logic with acquaintance that you have,
And practice rhetoric in your common talk;   35
Music and poesy use to quicken you;
The mathematics and the metaphysics—
Fall to them as you find your stomach serves you.
No profit grows where is no pleasure ta'en.
In brief, sir, study what you most affect.   40
LUCENTIO
Gramercies, Tranio, well dost thou advise.
If, Biondello, thou wert come ashore,
We could at once put us in readiness
And take a lodging fit to entertain
Such friends as time in Padua shall beget.   45

Enter Baptista with his two daughters, Katherine and
Bianca; Gremio, a pantaloon, ⌐*and*¬ *Hortensio,* ⌐*suitors*¬
to Bianca.

But stay awhile! What company is this?
TRANIO
Master, some show to welcome us to town.
                    Lucentio ⌐*and*¬ *Tranio stand by.*
BAPTISTA, ⌐*to Gremio and Hortensio*¬
Gentlemen, importune me no farther,
For how I firmly am resolved you know:

33

50. **bestow:** give in marriage
54. **Leave:** permission
55. **cart:** Women who transgressed community standards were shamed by being paraded through the streets in open carts.
58. **stale:** laughingstock; also prostitute (Prostitutes were among those "carted."); **mates:** fellows
59. **mates:** spouses
63. **Iwis:** certainly; **it:** i.e., marriage; **her:** i.e., Katherine's
65. **noddle:** head (slang)
66. **paint:** i.e., scratch until it bleeds
69. **pastime toward:** entertainment about to take place
70. **wonderful froward:** amazingly ungovernable

Pantaloon. (1.1.45 SD)
From Octavio van Veen,
Quinti Horatii Flacci emblemata (1612).

That is, not to bestow my youngest daughter   50
Before I have a husband for the elder.
If either of you both love Katherine,
Because I know you well and love you well,
Leave shall you have to court her at your pleasure.

GREMIO
To cart her, rather. She's too rough for me.—   55
There, there, Hortensio, will you any wife?

KATHERINE, ⌈to Baptista⌉
I pray you, sir, is it your will
To make a stale of me amongst these mates?

HORTENSIO
"Mates," maid? How mean you that? No mates for
    you,   60
Unless you were of gentler, milder mold.

KATHERINE
I' faith, sir, you shall never need to fear.
Iwis it is not halfway to her heart.
But if it were, doubt not her care should be
To comb your noddle with a three-legged stool   65
And paint your face and use you like a fool.

HORTENSIO
From all such devils, good Lord, deliver us!

GREMIO   And me too, good Lord.

TRANIO, ⌈aside to Lucentio⌉
Husht, master, here's some good pastime toward;
That wench is stark mad or wonderful froward.   70

LUCENTIO, ⌈aside to Tranio⌉
But in the other's silence do I see
Maid's mild behavior and sobriety.
Peace, Tranio.

TRANIO, ⌈aside to Lucentio⌉
Well said, master. Mum, and gaze your fill.

BAPTISTA, ⌈to Gremio and Hortensio⌉
Gentlemen, that I may soon make good   75
What I have said—Bianca, get you in,

35

79. **peat:** pet, favorite

79–80. **It is . . . why:** she should make herself cry, if she had some excuse

82. **subscribe:** give in, submit

83. **instruments:** musical instruments

85. **Minerva:** goddess of wisdom, also credited with inventing musical instruments

86. **strange:** uncooperative, unfriendly

89. **mew her up:** cage her

90. **for:** because of

91. **her . . . her:** i.e., Bianca . . . Katherine's

99. **Prefer:** recommend; **cunning:** learned

103. **commune:** talk over together

105. **belike:** as is probable

Minerva. (1.1.85)
From Ottavio Rossi,
La memoria bresciane . . . (1616).

And let it not displease thee, good Bianca,
For I will love thee ne'er the less, my girl.
KATHERINE
A pretty peat! It is best
Put finger in the eye, an she knew why.   80
BIANCA
Sister, content you in my discontent.—
Sir, to your pleasure humbly I subscribe.
My books and instruments shall be my company,
On them to look and practice by myself.
LUCENTIO, ⌜aside to Tranio⌝
Hark, Tranio, thou mayst hear Minerva speak!   85
HORTENSIO
Signior Baptista, will you be so strange?
Sorry am I that our goodwill effects
Bianca's grief.
GREMIO   Why will you mew her up,
Signior Baptista, for this fiend of hell,   90
And make her bear the penance of her tongue?
BAPTISTA
Gentlemen, content you. I am resolved.—
Go in, Bianca.   ⌜Bianca exits.⌝
And for I know she taketh most delight
In music, instruments, and poetry,   95
Schoolmasters will I keep within my house
Fit to instruct her youth. If you, Hortensio,
Or, Signior Gremio, you know any such,
Prefer them hither. For to cunning men
I will be very kind, and liberal   100
To mine own children in good bringing up.
And so, farewell.—Katherine, you may stay,
For I have more to commune with Bianca. *He exits.*
KATHERINE
Why, and I trust I may go too, may I not?
What, shall I be appointed hours as though, belike, 105
I knew not what to take and what to leave? Ha!
                              She exits.

107. **devil's dam:** devil's mother (in proverbs, said to be worse than the devil)

108. **hold:** restrain; **Their love:** perhaps, the love of women (Some editors print this as "There! Love . . .")

109. **blow our nails:** i.e., wait patiently

110–11. **Our cake's . . . sides:** proverbial for "we've both lost"

114. **wish:** recommend

117. **brooked parle:** i.e., allowed for discussion; **advice:** careful consideration; **toucheth:** concerns

126–27. **so very a fool:** entirely a fool as

129. **alarums:** brawlings

131. **light on:** i.e., find

132. **and:** if (there were)

133. **had as lief:** would just as soon

134. **high cross:** the cross at the town center

137. **bar in law:** legal barrier (i.e., Baptista's insistence that Katherine must be married before Bianca)

141. **have to 't afresh:** i.e., compete anew, go to it again

142. **Happy . . . dole:** i.e., may the winner find happiness; or, may the best man win

GREMIO You may go to the devil's dam! Your gifts are
so good here's none will hold you.—Their love is
not so great, Hortensio, but we may blow our nails
together and fast it fairly out. Our cake's dough on   110
both sides. Farewell. Yet for the love I bear my
sweet Bianca, if I can by any means light on a fit
man to teach her that wherein she delights, I will
wish him to her father.

HORTENSIO So will I, Signior Gremio. But a word, I   115
pray. Though the nature of our quarrel yet never
brooked parle, know now upon advice, it toucheth
us both (that we may yet again have access to our
fair mistress and be happy rivals in Bianca's love) to
labor and effect one thing specially.   120

GREMIO What's that, I pray?

HORTENSIO Marry, sir, to get a husband for her sister.

GREMIO A husband? A devil!

HORTENSIO I say "a husband."

GREMIO I say "a devil." Think'st thou, Hortensio,   125
though her father be very rich, any man is so very a
fool to be married to hell?

HORTENSIO Tush, Gremio. Though it pass your patience and mine to endure her loud alarums, why,
man, there be good fellows in the world, an a man   130
could light on them, would take her with all faults,
and money enough.

GREMIO I cannot tell. But I had as lief take her dowry
with this condition: to be whipped at the high cross
every morning.   135

HORTENSIO Faith, as you say, there's small choice in
rotten apples. But come, since this bar in law
makes us friends, it shall be so far forth friendly
maintained till by helping Baptista's eldest daughter to a husband we set his youngest free for a   140
husband, and then have to 't afresh. Sweet Bianca!
Happy man be his dole! He that runs fastest gets the
ring. How say you, Signior Gremio?

144–45. **would I . . . wooing:** i.e., I wish I had already given Katherine's wooer the best horse in Padua as encouragement to begin his wooing

153. **I found . . . love-in-idleness:** i.e., I fell in love (Lucentio plays with the idea that idleness begets amorous love, "love-in-idleness" being the name of a flower whose juice in one's eyes, according to Shakespeare's *A Midsummer Night's Dream*, causes one to love the next thing that one sees.)

155. **to me as secret:** as much in my confidence

156. **Anna to the Queen of Carthage:** In Virgil's *Aeneid*, Dido, queen of Carthage, has a sister, Anna, to whom the queen reveals her love for Aeneas.

162. **rated:** chided, scolded

164. **Redime . . . minimo:** i.e., ransom yourself from capture for as little money as possible

165. **Gramercies:** thanks; **contents:** i.e., makes me content

167. **longly:** long; perhaps also longingly

168. **marked not:** did not notice; **pith:** essence

170. **daughter of Agenor:** Europa, whom Jove, in the form of a bull, took to Crete (The story is told in Ovid's *Metamorphoses*.)

GREMIO   I am agreed, and would I had given him the
      best horse in Padua to begin his wooing that would   145
      thoroughly woo her, wed her, and bed her, and rid
      the house of her. Come on.
                              ⌈*Gremio and Hortensio*⌉ *exit.*
                          Tranio and Lucentio remain onstage.
TRANIO
   I pray, sir, tell me, is it possible
   That love should of a sudden take such hold?
LUCENTIO
   O Tranio, till I found it to be true,   150
   I never thought it possible or likely.
   But see, while idly I stood looking on,
   I found the effect of love-in-idleness,
   And now in plainness do confess to thee
   That art to me as secret and as dear   155
   As Anna to the Queen of Carthage was:
   Tranio, I burn, I pine! I perish, Tranio,
   If I achieve not this young modest girl.
   Counsel me, Tranio, for I know thou canst.
   Assist me, Tranio, for I know thou wilt.   160
TRANIO
   Master, it is no time to chide you now.
   Affection is not rated from the heart.
   If love have touched you, naught remains but so:
   Redime te ⌈*captum*⌉ *quam queas minimo.*
LUCENTIO
   Gramercies, lad. Go forward. This contents;   165
   The rest will comfort, for thy counsel's sound.
TRANIO
   Master, you looked so longly on the maid,
   Perhaps you marked not what's the pith of all.
LUCENTIO
   O yes, I saw sweet beauty in her face,
   Such as the daughter of Agenor had,   170
   That made great Jove to humble him to her hand
   When with his knees he kissed the Cretan strand.

176. **her:** i.e., Bianca's
183. **curst and shrewd:** bad-tempered and loud
186. **mewed:** caged
187. **Because:** i.e., so that
191. **'tis plotted:** i.e., I've a scheme
193. **for my hand:** i.e., I'll bet my hand
194. **meet . . . one:** i.e., coincide perfectly

Europa, "daughter of Agenor,"
borne by "great Jove." (1.1.170–71)
From Gabriele Simeoni, *La vita* . . . (1559).

TRANIO
Saw you no more? Marked you not how her sister
Began to scold and raise up such a storm
That mortal ears might hardly endure the din?   175
LUCENTIO
Tranio, I saw her coral lips to move,
And with her breath she did perfume the air.
Sacred and sweet was all I saw in her.
TRANIO, ⌈aside⌉
Nay, then 'tis time to stir him from his trance.—
I pray, awake, sir! If you love the maid,   180
Bend thoughts and wits to achieve her. Thus it
    stands:
Her elder sister is so curst and shrewd
That till the father rid his hands of her,
Master, your love must live a maid at home,   185
And therefore has he closely mewed her up,
Because she will not be annoyed with suitors.
LUCENTIO
Ah, Tranio, what a cruel father's he!
But art thou not advised he took some care
To get her cunning schoolmasters to instruct her?   190
TRANIO
Ay, marry, am I, sir—and now 'tis plotted!
LUCENTIO
I have it, Tranio!
TRANIO   Master, for my hand,
Both our inventions meet and jump in one.
LUCENTIO
Tell me thine first.   195
TRANIO   You will be schoolmaster
And undertake the teaching of the maid:
That's your device.
LUCENTIO   It is. May it be done?
TRANIO
Not possible. For who shall bear your part   200

43

202. **Keep house:** establish a household

204. **Basta:** Italian for "enough"; **have it full:** i.e., have worked out a whole plan

209. **port:** style of life fitting my station

211. **meaner:** less socially important

213. **Uncase thee:** i.e., undress

214. **waits on:** serves

215. **charm . . . tongue:** first conjure him to stay quiet

218. **tied:** bound, obligated

220. **quoth:** said

226. **Whose sudden sight:** i.e., the sudden sight of whom; **thralled:** enthralled, enslaved

And be in Padua here Vincentio's son,
Keep house, and ply his book, welcome his friends,
Visit his countrymen and banquet them?

LUCENTIO
Basta, content thee, for I have it full.
We have not yet been seen in any house,   205
Nor can we be distinguished by our faces
For man or master. Then it follows thus:
Thou shalt be master, Tranio, in my stead,
Keep house, and port, and servants, as I should.
I will some other be, some Florentine,   210
Some Neapolitan, or meaner man of Pisa.
'Tis hatched, and shall be so. Tranio, at once
Uncase thee. Take my colored hat and cloak.
⌐*They exchange clothes.*⌐
When Biondello comes, he waits on thee,
But I will charm him first to keep his tongue.   215

TRANIO   So had you need.
In brief, sir, sith it your pleasure is,
And I am tied to be obedient
(For so your father charged me at our parting:
"Be serviceable to my son," quoth he,   220
Although I think 'twas in another sense),
I am content to be Lucentio,
Because so well I love Lucentio.

LUCENTIO
Tranio, be so, because Lucentio loves,
And let me be a slave, t' achieve that maid   225
Whose sudden sight hath thralled my wounded eye.

Enter Biondello.

Here comes the rogue.—Sirrah, where have you
  been?

BIONDELLO
Where have I been? Nay, how now, where are you?

45

233. **frame:** adjust
235. **count'nance:** appearance, manner
236. **for:** i.e., to make good
238. **descried:** identified, recognized
239. **becomes:** is becoming or appropriate
242. **Ne'er a whit:** i.e., not a bit
255. **rests:** remains
256. **make:** become
258 SD. **Presenters:** characters in the Induction (who "presented" the play)
259. **mind:** pay attention to

Master, has my fellow Tranio stolen your clothes?   230
Or you stolen his? Or both? Pray, what's the news?
LUCENTIO
Sirrah, come hither. 'Tis no time to jest,
And therefore frame your manners to the time.
Your fellow, Tranio here, to save my life,
Puts my apparel and my count'nance on,   235
And I for my escape have put on his;
For in a quarrel since I came ashore
I killed a man and fear I was descried.
Wait you on him, I charge you, as becomes,
While I make way from hence to save my life.   240
You understand me?
BIONDELLO   Ay, sir. ⌜Aside.⌝ Ne'er a whit.
LUCENTIO
And not a jot of "Tranio" in your mouth.
Tranio is changed into Lucentio.
BIONDELLO
The better for him. Would I were so too.   245
TRANIO
So could I, faith, boy, to have the next wish after,
That Lucentio indeed had Baptista's youngest
    daughter.
But, sirrah, not for my sake, but your master's, I
    advise   250
You use your manners discreetly in all kind of
    companies.
When I am alone, why then I am Tranio;
But in all places else, ⌜your⌝ master Lucentio.
LUCENTIO   Tranio, let's go. One thing more rests, that   255
    thyself execute, to make one among these wooers. If
    thou ask me why, sufficeth my reasons are both
    good and weighty.   They exit.
                    The Presenters above ⌜speak.⌝
FIRST SERVINGMAN
My lord, you nod. You do not mind the play.

264. **Would:** i.e., I wish
264 SD. **mark:** i.e., watch

1.2 Petruchio, with his servant Grumio, has just arrived in Padua. His friend Hortensio suggests that Petruchio woo Katherine. Petruchio enthusiastically agrees. He agrees also to present Hortensio, in disguise, to Baptista as a music teacher named Litio. Gremio appears with Lucentio, who is disguised as a teacher named Cambio. Last of all comes Tranio, now impersonating Lucentio and declaring his intention to woo Bianca. Gremio, Hortensio, and Tranio (as Lucentio) agree to help Petruchio win Katherine.

0 SD. **man:** i.e., servant
2. **of all:** especially
3. **approvèd:** tried, tested
4. **trow:** think
7. **rebused:** Grumio's error for "abused"
8. **knock me:** i.e., knock (rap on the gate) for me (Grumio takes **me** to be the object of **knock,** and continues to define **knock me** as "hit me.")
12. **pate:** head
13–15. **I . . . worst:** i.e., if I were to hit you first, I know who would afterward get the worst of it
17. **ring it:** perhaps, use the ring fastened to the door as a knocker (with a pun on "wring")
18. **sol, fa:** notes on the scale; **sing it:** i.e., wail

SLY   Yes, by Saint Anne, do I. A good matter, surely.   260
    Comes there any more of it?
⌜PAGE, *as*⌝ LADY   My lord, 'tis but begun.
SLY   'Tis a very excellent piece of work, madam lady.
    Would 'twere done.

                               They sit and mark.

                 ⌜Scene 2⌝
      Enter Petruchio and his man Grumio.

PETRUCHIO
    Verona, for a while I take my leave
    To see my friends in Padua, but of all
    My best belovèd and approvèd friend,
    Hortensio. And I trow this is his house.
    Here, sirrah Grumio, knock, I say.   5
GRUMIO   Knock, sir? Whom should I knock? Is there
    any man has rebused your Worship?
PETRUCHIO   Villain, I say, knock me here soundly.
GRUMIO   Knock you here, sir? Why, sir, what am I, sir,
    that I should knock you here, sir?   10
PETRUCHIO
    Villain, I say, knock me at this gate
    And rap me well, or I'll knock your knave's pate.
GRUMIO
    My master is grown quarrelsome. I should knock
      you first,
    And then I know after who comes by the worst.   15
PETRUCHIO   Will it not be?
    Faith, sirrah, an you'll not knock, I'll ring it.
    I'll try how you can *sol*, *fa*, and sing it.
          He wrings him by the ears. ⌜*Grumio falls.*⌝
GRUMIO   Help, mistress, help! My master is mad.
PETRUCHIO   Now knock when I bid you, sirrah   20
    villain.

                     49

25. **part the fray:** i.e., stop the fight

26. **Con tutto il cuore ben trovato:** Italian for "Well found (i.e., welcome) with all [my] heart"

27–28. **Alla . . . Petruchio:** Italian for "Welcome to our house, my much honored Master Petruchio"

29. **compound:** settle

30. **'leges:** i.e., alleges

31. **Latin:** Grumio seems to be presented as an Englishman who cannot tell the difference between Italian and Latin.

35. **two-and-thirty . . . out:** i.e., not quite right in the head (The allusion is to a card game called "one-in-thirty." According to Grumio, Petruchio is one "pip"—i.e., one mark on the card—over the goal of the game.)

46. **pledge:** guarantor

47. **this':** i.e., this is; **heavy chance:** grave misfortune

48. **ancient:** long-time

Enter Hortensio.

HORTENSIO How now, what's the matter? My old
friend Grumio and my good friend Petruchio? How
do you all at Verona?

PETRUCHIO
Signior Hortensio, come you to part the fray?   25
⌐*Con tutto il cuore ben trovato,*⌐ may I say.

HORTENSIO *Alla nostra casa* ⌐*ben*⌐ *venuto,* ⌐*molto
honorato*⌐ *signor mio Petruchio.*—Rise, Grumio,
rise. We will compound this quarrel. ⌐*Grumio rises.*⌐

GRUMIO Nay, 'tis no matter, sir, what he 'leges in   30
Latin. If this be not a lawful cause for me to leave
his service—look you, sir: he bid me knock him
and rap him soundly, sir. Well, was it fit for a
servant to use his master so, being perhaps, for
aught I see, two-and-thirty, a pip out?   35
Whom, would to God, I had well knocked at first,
Then had not Grumio come by the worst.

PETRUCHIO
A senseless villain, good Hortensio.
I bade the rascal knock upon your gate
And could not get him for my heart to do it.   40

GRUMIO Knock at the gate? O, heavens, spake you not
these words plain: "Sirrah, knock me here, rap me
here, knock me well, and knock me soundly"? And
come you now with "knocking at the gate"?

PETRUCHIO
Sirrah, begone, or talk not, I advise you.   45

HORTENSIO
Petruchio, patience. I am Grumio's pledge.
Why, this' a heavy chance 'twixt him and you,
Your ancient, trusty, pleasant servant Grumio.
And tell me now, sweet friend, what happy gale
Blows you to Padua here from old Verona?   50

PETRUCHIO
Such wind as scatters young men through the world

51

53. **in a few:** i.e., in a few words
56. **maze:** intricate puzzle (See page 60.)
57. **Happily:** perhaps; or, with pleasure
58. **Crowns:** i.e., coins
60. **come roundly to thee:** speak to you bluntly
61. **ill-favored:** unattractive (because bad-tempered)
69. **burden:** refrain; or, bass accompaniment
70. **foul:** ugly; **Florentius' love:** Florentius, in John Gower's fourteenth-century *Confessio Amantis*, agrees to marry an old hag, who is later transformed into a young beauty.
71. **Sibyl:** the Sibyl of Cumae, granted as many years of life as there are grains in a handful of sand; **curst and shrewd:** bad-tempered
72. **Socrates' Xanthippe:** The wife of Socrates is usually represented as a shrew.
73. **moves:** disturbs, dislodges
80. **aglet-baby:** i.e., doll decked with spangles
81. **trot:** hag
83. **withal:** with it

To seek their fortunes farther than at home,
Where small experience grows. But in a few,
Signior Hortensio, thus it stands with me:
Antonio, my father, is deceased,   55
And I have thrust myself into this maze,
Happily to wive and thrive, as best I may.
Crowns in my purse I have and goods at home,
And so am come abroad to see the world.

HORTENSIO
Petruchio, shall I then come roundly to thee   60
And wish thee to a shrewd ill-favored wife?
Thou'dst thank me but a little for my counsel—
And yet I'll promise thee she shall be rich,
And very rich. But thou'rt too much my friend,
And I'll not wish thee to her.   65

PETRUCHIO
Signior Hortensio, 'twixt such friends as we
Few words suffice. And therefore, if thou know
One rich enough to be Petruchio's wife
(As wealth is burden of my wooing dance),
Be she as foul as was Florentius' love,   70
As old as Sibyl, and as curst and shrewd
As Socrates' Xanthippe, or a worse,
She moves me not, or not removes at least
Affection's edge in me, were she as rough
As are the swelling Adriatic seas.   75
I come to wive it wealthily in Padua;
If wealthily, then happily in Padua.

GRUMIO, ⌈to Hortensio⌉   Nay, look you, sir, he tells you
    flatly what his mind is. Why, give him gold enough
    and marry him to a puppet or an aglet-baby, or an   80
    old trot with ne'er a tooth in her head, though she
    have as many diseases as two-and-fifty horses. Why,
    nothing comes amiss, so money comes withal.

HORTENSIO
Petruchio, since we are stepped thus far in,

85. **that:** i.e., that which

91. **shrewd, and froward:** shrewish and perverse

92. **state:** financial status

96. **board her:** i.e., woo her

106. **give you over:** leave you right now

109. **humor:** whim, mood

111–12. **half a score:** ten

113. **rail . . . tricks:** perhaps, scold in his "rhetorics"; or, use abusive language for which he should be hanged (The passage is very obscure.)

114. **stand him:** i.e., stand up to him (with a sexual meaning as well)

114–17. These lines suggest that Petruchio will throw "figures of speech" at Katherine until she is overcome. But they also suggest physical violence, and, perhaps, rape.

The Sibyl of Cumae. (1.2.71)
From Philippus de Barberiis, *Quattuor hic compressa . . .* (1495).

I will continue that I broached in jest.   85
I can, Petruchio, help thee to a wife
With wealth enough, and young and beauteous,
Brought up as best becomes a gentlewoman.
Her only fault, and that is faults enough,
Is that she is intolerable curst,   90
And shrewd, and froward, so beyond all measure
That, were my state far worser than it is,
I would not wed her for a mine of gold.

PETRUCHIO
Hortensio, peace. Thou know'st not gold's effect.
Tell me her father's name, and 'tis enough;   95
For I will board her, though she chide as loud
As thunder when the clouds in autumn crack.

HORTENSIO
Her father is Baptista Minola,
An affable and courteous gentleman.
Her name is Katherina Minola,   100
Renowned in Padua for her scolding tongue.

PETRUCHIO
I know her father, though I know not her,
And he knew my deceasèd father well.
I will not sleep, Hortensio, till I see her,
And therefore let me be thus bold with you   105
To give you over at this first encounter—
Unless you will accompany me thither.

GRUMIO, ⌜to Hortensio⌝ I pray you, sir, let him go while
the humor lasts. O' my word, an she knew him as
well as I do, she would think scolding would do little   110
good upon him. She may perhaps call him half a
score knaves or so. Why, that's nothing; an he begin
once, he'll rail in his rope tricks. I'll tell you what,
sir, an she stand him but a little, he will throw a
figure in her face and so disfigure her with it that   115
she shall have no more eyes to see withal than a cat.
You know him not, sir.

118. **Tarry:** wait

119. **keep:** i.e., keeping; or, castle keep, the heavily fortified inner tower of a castle

120. **hold:** i.e., his stronghold; safekeeping

122. **other more:** i.e., others too

124. **Supposing:** i.e., Baptista supposes

125. **For:** i.e., because of; **rehearsed:** itemized

127. **this . . . ta'en:** i.e., Baptista has arranged

132. **do me grace:** do me a favor

133. **sober:** dark

135. **Well seen:** well trained

136. **device:** scheme

137. **leave:** opportunity; **make love to:** pay amorous attention to, woo

144. **proper stripling:** handsome youngster (sarcastic reference to Gremio)

A scholar in "sober robes." (1.2.133)
From Geoffrey Whitney, *A choice of emblemes* (1586).

HORTENSIO
Tarry, Petruchio. I must go with thee,
For in Baptista's keep my treasure is.
He hath the jewel of my life in hold,   120
His youngest daughter, beautiful Bianca,
And her withholds from me ⌜and⌝ other more,
Suitors to her and rivals in my love,
Supposing it a thing impossible,
For those defects I have before rehearsed,   125
That ever Katherina will be wooed.
Therefore this order hath Baptista ta'en,
That none shall have access unto Bianca
Till Katherine the curst have got a husband.
GRUMIO "Katherine the curst,"   130
A title for a maid, of all titles the worst.
HORTENSIO
Now shall my friend Petruchio do me grace
And offer me disguised in sober robes
To old Baptista as a schoolmaster
Well seen in music, to instruct Bianca,   135
That so I may, by this device at least,
Have leave and leisure to make love to her
And unsuspected court her by herself.
GRUMIO Here's no knavery! See, to beguile the old
folks, how the young folks lay their heads together! 140

*Enter Gremio and Lucentio, disguised ⌜as Cambio, a
schoolmaster.⌝*

Master, master, look about you. Who goes there, ha?
HORTENSIO
Peace, Grumio, it is the rival of my love.
Petruchio, stand by awhile.
        ⌜*Petruchio, Hortensio, and Grumio stand aside.*⌝
GRUMIO, ⌜*aside*⌝
A proper stripling, and an amorous.

57

145. **the note:** i.e., perhaps, a list of the books mentioned at line 147

146. **bound:** books were sold unbound

147. **See . . . hand:** i.e., see to that in any case

148. **lectures:** lessons

150. **liberality:** generosity; probably, here, "what Baptista pays you"

151. **mend:** improve; **a largess:** a gift of money; **paper:** probably the note mentioned above

152. **them:** i.e., the books

156. **stand:** i.e., rest

157. **as yourself . . . place:** as if you were present the whole time

161. **woodcock:** i.e., dupe (A woodcock is a bird easily snared and therefore thought to be foolish.)

166. **Trow:** know

172. **warrant:** guarantee

GREMIO, ⌜to Lucentio⌝
  O, very well, I have perused the note.   145
  Hark you, sir, I'll have them very fairly bound,
  All books of love. See that at any hand,
  And see you read no other lectures to her.
  You understand me. Over and beside
  Signior Baptista's liberality,   150
  I'll mend it with a largess. Take your paper too.
  And let me have them very well perfumed,
  For she is sweeter than perfume itself
  To whom they go to. What will you read to her?
LUCENTIO, ⌜as CAMBIO⌝
  Whate'er I read to her, I'll plead for you   155
  As for my patron, stand you so assured,
  As firmly as yourself were still in place,
  Yea, and perhaps with more successful words
  Than you—unless you were a scholar, sir.
GREMIO
  O this learning, what a thing it is!   160
GRUMIO, ⌜aside⌝
  O this woodcock, what an ass it is!
PETRUCHIO, ⌜aside⌝   Peace, sirrah.
HORTENSIO, ⌜aside⌝
  Grumio, mum.   ⌜Coming forward.⌝
              God save you, Signior Gremio.
GREMIO
  And you are well met, Signior Hortensio.   165
  Trow you whither I am going? To Baptista Minola.
  I promised to enquire carefully
  About a schoolmaster for the fair Bianca,
  And by good fortune I have lighted well
  On this young man, for learning and behavior   170
  Fit for her turn, well read in poetry
  And other books—good ones, I warrant you.
HORTENSIO
  'Tis well. And I have met a gentleman

179. **bags:** i.e., moneybags
180. **vent:** express
181. **fair:** courteously
182. **indifferent:** equally
184. **Upon agreement . . . liking:** i.e., if we agree to terms that he likes (Hortensio and Gremio are to pay the expenses that Petruchio incurs in his courtship of Katherine; see lines 218–19.)
187. **So said, so done, is well:** i.e., if the deeds match the words, this is good
191. **What countryman?:** i.e., from what country are you?
196. **stomach:** desire, spirit, courage; **to 't:** go to it; **i':** i.e., in

A maze. (1.2.56)
From Claude Paradin, *Devises héroïques* . . . (1557).

Hath promised me to help ⌜me⌝ to another,
A fine musician to instruct our mistress.   175
So shall I no whit be behind in duty
To fair Bianca, so beloved of me.
GREMIO
Beloved of me, and that my deeds shall prove.
GRUMIO, ⌜aside⌝   And that his bags shall prove.
HORTENSIO
Gremio, 'tis now no time to vent our love.   180
Listen to me, and if you speak me fair
I'll tell you news indifferent good for either.
                         ⌜Presenting Petruchio.⌝
Here is a gentleman whom by chance I met,
Upon agreement from us to his liking,
Will undertake to woo curst Katherine,   185
Yea, and to marry her, if her dowry please.
GREMIO   So said, so done, is well.
Hortensio, have you told him all her faults?
PETRUCHIO
I know she is an irksome, brawling scold.
If that be all, masters, I hear no harm.   190
GREMIO
No? Sayst me so, friend? What countryman?
PETRUCHIO
Born in Verona, old Antonio's son.
My father dead, my fortune lives for me,
And I do hope good days and long to see.
GREMIO
Oh, sir, such a life with such a wife were strange.   195
But if you have a stomach, to 't, i' God's name!
You shall have me assisting you in all.
But will you woo this wildcat?
PETRUCHIO   Will I live?
GRUMIO
Will he woo her? Ay, or I'll hang her.   200

206. **ordnance:** heavy guns

209. **'larums:** i.e., alarums, or calls to battle

213. **fear boys with bugs:** frighten little boys with bugbears or bogeymen

216. **happily:** opportunely, at just the right time

219. **bear . . . of:** pay his expenses for

223. **readiest:** i.e., shortest

225. **fair:** beautiful

228. **her to—:** Gremio seems to be interrupted here before he finishes the question "you mean not her to woo?" (Some editors print the line as "mean not her too?")

A "chestnut in a farmer's fire." (1.2.212)
From Jacob Cats, *Alle de werken* . . . (1657–59).

PETRUCHIO
  Why came I hither but to that intent?
  Think you a little din can daunt mine ears?
  Have I not in my time heard lions roar?
  Have I not heard the sea, puffèd up with winds,
  Rage like an angry boar chafèd with sweat?   205
  Have I not heard great ordnance in the field
  And heaven's artillery thunder in the skies?
  Have I not in a pitchèd battle heard
  Loud 'larums, neighing steeds, and trumpets clang?
  And do you tell me of a woman's tongue,   210
  That gives not half so great a blow to hear
  As will a chestnut in a farmer's fire?
  Tush, tush, fear boys with bugs!
GRUMIO   For he fears none.
GREMIO Hortensio, hark.   215
  This gentleman is happily arrived,
  My mind presumes, for his own good and yours.
HORTENSIO
  I promised we would be contributors
  And bear his charge of wooing whatsoe'er.
GREMIO
  And so we will, provided that he win her.   220
GRUMIO
  I would I were as sure of a good dinner.

Enter Tranio, ⌜disguised as Lucentio,⌝ and Biondello.

TRANIO, ⌜*as* LUCENTIO⌝
  Gentlemen, God save you. If I may be bold,
  Tell me, I beseech you, which is the readiest way
  To the house of Signior Baptista Minola?
BIONDELLO He that has the two fair daughters—is 't   225
  he you mean?
TRANIO, ⌜*as* LUCENTIO⌝ Even he, Biondello.
GREMIO
  Hark you, sir, you mean not her to—

229. **What . . . do?:** i.e., what business is it of yours?

230. **her that chides:** i.e., Katherine; **at any hand:** in any case

233. **ere:** before

236. **get you hence:** i.e., go away

242. **choice:** i.e., chosen

244. **Softly:** gently

248. **And were his daughter fairer:** We would probably say: "Even if she were less fair than she is."

250. **Leda's daughter:** the legendarily beautiful Helen of Troy, daughter of the god Jove and the woman Leda

251. **well . . . have:** i.e., Bianca may well have one more

252. **make one:** i.e., be one

253. **Paris:** lover of Helen of Troy; **speed:** prevail, succeed

TRANIO, ⌜as LUCENTIO⌝
  Perhaps him and her, sir. What have you to do?
PETRUCHIO
  Not her that chides, sir, at any hand, I pray.   230
TRANIO, ⌜as LUCENTIO⌝
  I love no chiders, sir. Biondello, let's away.
LUCENTIO, ⌜aside⌝
  Well begun, Tranio.
HORTENSIO   Sir, a word ere you go.
  Are you a suitor to the maid you talk of, yea or no?
TRANIO, ⌜as LUCENTIO⌝
  An if I be, sir, is it any offense?   235
GREMIO
  No, if without more words you will get you hence.
TRANIO, ⌜as LUCENTIO⌝
  Why sir, I pray, are not the streets as free
  For me, as for you?
GREMIO   But so is not she.
TRANIO, ⌜as LUCENTIO⌝
  For what reason, I beseech you?   240
GREMIO
  For this reason, if you'll know:
  That she's the choice love of Signior Gremio.
HORTENSIO
  That she's the chosen of Signior Hortensio.
TRANIO, ⌜as LUCENTIO⌝
  Softly, my masters. If you be gentlemen,
  Do me this right: hear me with patience.   245
  Baptista is a noble gentleman
  To whom my father is not all unknown,
  And were his daughter fairer than she is,
  She may more suitors have, and me for one.
  Fair Leda's daughter had a thousand wooers.   250
  Then well one more may fair Bianca have.
  And so she shall. Lucentio shall make one,
  Though Paris came in hope to speed alone.

254. **What:** an interjection introducing a question or an exclamation

255. **give him head:** i.e., let him run (as if he were a horse); **jade:** a worthless horse

257. **as:** i.e., as to

262. **let her go by:** leave her alone

263. **Hercules:** Also called Alcides, he was required to undertake twelve seemingly impossible labors.

266. **hearken:** ask

272. **stead:** help

275. **hap:** fortune

276. **so graceless . . . ingrate:** i.e., be so ungracious as to be ungrateful

277. **conceive:** understand

279. **gratify:** i.e., pay

A jade. (1.2.255)
From Cesare Fiaschi, *Trattato dell'imbrigliare* . . . (1614).

GREMIO
  What, this gentleman will out-talk us all!
LUCENTIO, ⌜as CAMBIO⌝
  Sir, give him head; I know he'll prove a jade.   255
PETRUCHIO
  Hortensio, to what end are all these words?
HORTENSIO, ⌜to Tranio⌝
  Sir, let me be so bold as ask you,
  Did you yet ever see Baptista's daughter?
TRANIO, ⌜as LUCENTIO⌝
  No, sir, but hear I do that he hath two,
  The one as famous for a scolding tongue   260
  As is the other for beauteous modesty.
PETRUCHIO
  Sir, sir, the first's for me; let her go by.
GREMIO
  Yea, leave that labor to great Hercules,
  And let it be more than Alcides' twelve.
PETRUCHIO, ⌜to Tranio⌝
  Sir, understand you this of me, in sooth: 265
  The youngest daughter, whom you hearken for,
  Her father keeps from all access of suitors
  And will not promise her to any man
  Until the elder sister first be wed.
  The younger then is free, and not before.   270
TRANIO, ⌜as LUCENTIO⌝
  If it be so, sir, that you are the man
  Must stead us all, and me amongst the rest,
  And if you break the ice and do this ⌜feat,⌝
  Achieve the elder, set the younger free
  For our access, whose hap shall be to have her   275
  Will not so graceless be to be ingrate.
HORTENSIO
  Sir, you say well, and well you do conceive.
  And since you do profess to be a suitor,
  You must, as we do, gratify this gentleman,
  To whom we all rest generally beholding.   280

282. **Please . . . contrive:** i.e., if it please you, let us spend

283. **quaff carouses:** drink copiously

286. **motion:** proposal

288. **I . . . venuto:** i.e., I will introduce you; I will ensure your welcome

TRANIO, ⌜as LUCENTIO⌝
  Sir, I shall not be slack; in sign whereof,
  Please you we may contrive this afternoon
  And quaff carouses to our mistress' health,
  And do as adversaries do in law,
  Strive mightily, but eat and drink as friends.   285
GRUMIO ⌜and⌝ BIONDELLO
  O excellent motion! Fellows, let's be gone.
HORTENSIO
  The motion's good indeed, and be it so.—
  Petruchio, I shall be your ⌜ben⌝ venuto.

                           They exit.

THE
TAMING
OF THE
SHREW

ACT 2

2.1 Baptista stops Katherine from abusing Bianca and receives a visit from Petruchio, who presents Hortensio (disguised as Litio, a music teacher); Gremio introduces Lucentio (disguised as Cambio, a teacher of languages). Tranio, impersonating Lucentio, announces his wish to marry Bianca, and Petruchio his desire to marry Katherine. Baptista insists that Petruchio must get Katherine's love. Petruchio and Katherine, left alone, enter into a furious bout of wordplay. Petruchio then lies to Baptista, insisting that Katherine loves him but that the couple have agreed that she will pretend to dislike him in public. Katherine's wedding is arranged, and Baptista hears the offers that Gremio and Tranio (as Lucentio) make for Bianca. Tranio-Lucentio outbids Gremio and is awarded Bianca, provided that Vincentio, Lucentio's father, will guarantee the dowry. Tranio-Lucentio sets out to find someone to impersonate Vincentio and provide the guarantee.

---

2. **bondmaid:** same as slave
3. **goods:** things; articles of clothing
4. **Unbind:** i.e., if you will unbind
8. **charge:** command
13. **Minion:** hussy
14. **affect:** like
15. **but . . . him:** i.e., but in any case you shall have him
16. **belike:** perhaps
17. **fair:** i.e., in beautiful clothes

⌜ACT 2⌝

⌜Scene 1⌝

Enter Katherine and Bianca ⌜with her hands tied.⌝

BIANCA
Good sister, wrong me not, nor wrong yourself,
To make a bondmaid and a slave of me.
That I disdain. But for these other goods—
Unbind my hands, I'll pull them off myself,
Yea, all my raiment to my petticoat,   5
Or what you will command me will I do,
So well I know my duty to my elders.
KATHERINE
Of all thy suitors here I charge ⌜thee⌝ tell
Whom thou lov'st best. See thou dissemble not.
BIANCA
Believe me, sister, of all the men alive   10
I never yet beheld that special face
Which I could fancy more than any other.
KATHERINE
Minion, thou liest. Is 't not Hortensio?
BIANCA
If you affect him, sister, here I swear
I'll plead for you myself, but you shall have him.   15
KATHERINE
O, then belike you fancy riches more.
You will have Gremio to keep you fair.

73

18. **envy:** hate (pronounced "en-vigh' ")
27. **hilding:** beast
32. **flouts:** mocks, insults
34. **suffer me:** allow me to be, tolerate me
36. **dance . . . day:** the proverbial misfortune of the unmarried elder daughter on her sister's wedding day
37. **for:** because of; **lead . . . hell:** the proverbial fate of unmarried women

BIANCA
Is it for him you do envy me so?
Nay, then, you jest, and now I well perceive
You have but jested with me all this while.   20
I prithee, sister Kate, untie my hands.
                    ⌜*Katherine*⌝ *strikes her.*

KATHERINE
If that be jest, then all the rest was so.

                    Enter Baptista.

BAPTISTA
Why, how now, dame, whence grows this
    insolence?—
Bianca, stand aside.—Poor girl, she weeps!   25
                    ⌜*He unties her hands.*⌝
⌜*To Bianca.*⌝ Go ply thy needle; meddle not with her.
⌜*To Katherine.*⌝ For shame, thou hilding of a devilish
    spirit!
Why dost thou wrong her that did ne'er wrong
    thee?   30
When did she cross thee with a bitter word?

KATHERINE
Her silence flouts me, and I'll be revenged!
                    ⌜*She*⌝ *flies after Bianca.*

BAPTISTA
What, in my sight?—Bianca, get thee in.
                    ⌜*Bianca*⌝ *exits.*

KATHERINE
What, will you not suffer me? Nay, now I see
She is your treasure, she must have a husband,   35
I must dance barefoot on her wedding day
And, for your love to her, lead apes in hell.
Talk not to me. I will go sit and weep
Till I can find occasion of revenge.   ⌜*She exits.*⌝

BAPTISTA
Was ever gentleman thus grieved as I?   40
But who comes here?

41 SD. **mean man:** man of low status
49. **Give me leave:** permit me to continue
57. **entrance:** price of admission; **entertainment:** reception as a guest
62. **Accept of:** i.e., accept

Enter Gremio; Lucentio ⌐disguised as Cambio¬
in the habit of a mean man; Petruchio with
⌐Hortensio disguised as Litio; and¬ Tranio ⌐disguised
as Lucentio,¬ with his boy, ⌐Biondello,¬ bearing a lute
and books.

GREMIO Good morrow, neighbor Baptista.

BAPTISTA Good morrow, neighbor Gremio.—God
save you, gentlemen.

PETRUCHIO
And you, good sir. Pray, have you not a daughter   45
Called Katherina, fair and virtuous?

BAPTISTA
I have a daughter, sir, called Katherina.

GREMIO, ⌐*to Petruchio*¬
You are too blunt. Go to it orderly.

PETRUCHIO
You wrong me, Signior Gremio. Give me leave.—
I am a gentleman of Verona, sir,   50
That hearing of her beauty and her wit,
Her affability and bashful modesty,
Her wondrous qualities and mild behavior,
Am bold to show myself a forward guest
Within your house, to make mine eye the witness   55
Of that report which I so oft have heard,
And, for an entrance to my entertainment,
I do present you with a man of mine,
               ⌐*Presenting Hortensio, disguised as Litio.*¬
Cunning in music and the mathematics,
To instruct her fully in those sciences,   60
Whereof I know she is not ignorant.
Accept of him, or else you do me wrong.
His name is Litio, born in Mantua.

BAPTISTA
You're welcome, sir, and he for your good sake.

77

66. **is not for your turn:** i.e., is not right for you
68. **like not of:** i.e., do not like
74. **Saving:** with all respect to
76. **Bacare:** corrupt Latin for "get back"
77. **fain:** rather
80. **gift:** i.e., Litio, given to Baptista by Petruchio;
very grateful: i.e., for which you are very grateful
86. **the other:** i.e., Litio

But for my daughter Katherine, this I know,   65
She is not for your turn, the more my grief.

PETRUCHIO
I see you do not mean to part with her,
Or else you like not of my company.

BAPTISTA
Mistake me not. I speak but as I find.
Whence are you, sir? What may I call your name?   70

PETRUCHIO
Petruchio is my name, Antonio's son,
A man well known throughout all Italy.

BAPTISTA
I know him well. You are welcome for his sake.

GREMIO
Saving your tale, Petruchio, I pray
Let us that are poor petitioners speak too!   75
Bacare, you are marvelous forward.

PETRUCHIO
O, pardon me, Signior Gremio, I would fain be
    doing.

GREMIO
I doubt it not, sir. But you will curse your wooing.
    ⌜*To Baptista.* Neighbor,⌝ this is a gift very grateful,   80
I am sure of it. To express the like kindness, myself,
that have been more kindly beholding to you than
any, freely give unto ⌜you⌝ this young scholar ⌜*pre-
senting Lucentio, disguised as Cambio*⌝ that hath
been long studying at Rheims, as cunning in Greek,   85
Latin, and other languages as the other in music and
mathematics. His name is Cambio. Pray accept his
service.

BAPTISTA A thousand thanks, Signior Gremio. Wel-
    come, good Cambio. ⌜*To Tranio as Lucentio.*⌝ But,   90
    gentle sir, methinks you walk like a stranger. May I
    be so bold to know the cause of your coming?

79

98. **In the preferment of:** granting precedence to
116. **them both:** i.e., Katherine and Bianca
118. **orchard:** garden
119. **passing:** very

Apollo. (IND.2.35)
From Johann Herold, *Heydenwelt* (1554).

TRANIO, ⌜*as* LUCENTIO⌝
Pardon me, sir, the boldness is mine own,
That being a stranger in this city here
Do make myself a suitor to your daughter,   95
Unto Bianca, fair and virtuous.
Nor is your firm resolve unknown to me,
In the preferment of the eldest sister.
This liberty is all that I request,
That, upon knowledge of my parentage,   100
I may have welcome 'mongst the rest that woo
And free access and favor as the rest.
And toward the education of your daughters
I here bestow a simple instrument
And this small packet of Greek and Latin books.   105
          ⌜*Biondello comes forward with the gifts.*⌝
If you accept them, then their worth is great.
BAPTISTA
Lucentio is your name. Of whence, I pray?
TRANIO, ⌜*as* LUCENTIO⌝
Of Pisa, sir, son to Vincentio.
BAPTISTA
A mighty man of Pisa. By report
I know him well. You are very welcome, sir.   110
⌜*To Hortensio as Litio.*⌝ Take you the lute, ⌜*To*
    Lucentio as Cambio.⌝ and you the set of books.
You shall go see your pupils presently.
Holla, within!

                   Enter a Servant

          Sirrah, lead these gentlemen   115
To my daughters, and tell them both
These are their tutors. Bid them use them well.
          ⌜*Servant exits with Hortensio and Lucentio.*⌝
We will go walk a little in the orchard,
And then to dinner. You are passing welcome,
And so I pray you all to think yourselves.   120

                         81

129. **in possession:** for immediate possession

131. **widowhood:** her rights as a widow; **be it:** i.e., if it be

133. **specialties:** special contracts

134. **on either hand:** i.e., on both sides

145. **happy:** fortunate; **speed:** progress

147. **to the proof:** (1) in strong armor; (2) to the test

147–48. **as mountains . . . perpetually:** i.e., as mountains, which do not shake, even though winds blow against them perpetually

PETRUCHIO
  Signior Baptista, my business asketh haste,
  And every day I cannot come to woo.
  You knew my father well, and in him me,
  Left solely heir to all his lands and goods,
  Which I have bettered rather than decreased.   125
  Then tell me, if I get your daughter's love,
  What dowry shall I have with her to wife?
BAPTISTA
  After my death, the one half of my lands,
  And, in possession, twenty thousand crowns.
PETRUCHIO
  And, for that dowry, I'll assure her of   130
  Her widowhood, be it that she survive me,
  In all my lands and leases whatsoever.
  Let specialties be therefore drawn between us,
  That covenants may be kept on either hand.
BAPTISTA
  Ay, when the special thing is well obtained,   135
  That is, her love, for that is all in all.
PETRUCHIO
  Why, that is nothing. For I tell you, father,
  I am as peremptory as she proud-minded;
  And where two raging fires meet together,
  They do consume the thing that feeds their fury.   140
  Though little fire grows great with little wind,
  Yet extreme gusts will blow out fire and all.
  So I to her and so she yields to me,
  For I am rough and woo not like a babe.
BAPTISTA
  Well mayst thou woo, and happy be thy speed.   145
  But be thou armed for some unhappy words.
PETRUCHIO
  Ay, to the proof, as mountains are for winds,
  That shakes not, though they blow perpetually.

153. **hold with her:** withstand her use

154. **break:** tame, train

155. **broke the lute:** Usually in productions Hortensio enters with the lute broken over his head.

156. **did but tell:** only told; **mistook her frets:** placed her fingers the wrong way on the ridges or bars (**frets**) on the neck of the lute

159. **fume:** rage (as in "frets and fumes")

162. **pate:** head

163. **amazèd:** astounded

166. **Jack:** rascal

167. **As had she:** i.e., as if she had

168. **lusty:** lively

173. **apt:** inclined

A lute. (2.1.111)
From Silvestro Pietrasanta,
Symbola heroica . . . (1682).

Enter Hortensio ⌜as Litio⌝ with his head broke.

BAPTISTA
How now, my friend, why dost thou look so pale?
HORTENSIO, ⌜as LITIO⌝
For fear, I promise you, if I look pale.   150
BAPTISTA
What, will my daughter prove a good musician?
HORTENSIO, ⌜as LITIO⌝
I think she'll sooner prove a soldier!
Iron may hold with her, but never lutes.
BAPTISTA
Why, then thou canst not break her to the lute?
HORTENSIO, ⌜as LITIO⌝
Why, no, for she hath broke the lute to me.   155
I did but tell her she mistook her frets,
And bowed her hand to teach her fingering,
When, with a most impatient devilish spirit,
" 'Frets' call you these?" quoth she. "I'll fume with
   them!"   160
And with that word she struck me on the head,
And through the instrument my pate made way,
And there I stood amazèd for a while,
As on a pillory, looking through the lute,
While she did call me "rascal fiddler,"   165
And "twangling Jack," with twenty such vile terms,
As had she studied to misuse me so.
PETRUCHIO
Now, by the world, it is a lusty wench.
I love her ten times more than e'er I did.
O, how I long to have some chat with her!   170
BAPTISTA, ⌜to Hortensio as Litio⌝
Well, go with me, and be not so discomfited.
Proceed in practice with my younger daughter.
She's apt to learn, and thankful for good turns.—
Signior Petruchio, will you go with us,
Or shall I send my daughter Kate to you?   175

176. **attend:** await
178. **rail:** scold; **plain:** directly, simply
185. **pack:** i.e., pack up and leave
187. **deny:** refuse; **crave the day:** beg her to name the day
191. **but:** i.e., but you are
194. **curst:** ill-tempered, quarrelsome
196. **super-dainty:** especially choice, precious
197. **dainties:** delicacies to eat, also called "cates"
200. **sounded:** (1) spoken of; (2) measured for depth—hence **deeply** in the next line
202. **moved:** inspired
203. **in good time:** indeed

PETRUCHIO
I pray you do. I'll attend her here—
                                        All but Petruchio exit.
And woo her with some spirit when she comes!
Say that she rail, why then I'll tell her plain
She sings as sweetly as a nightingale.
Say that she frown, I'll say she looks as clear   180
As morning roses newly washed with dew.
Say she be mute and will not speak a word,
Then I'll commend her volubility
And say she uttereth piercing eloquence.
If she do bid me pack, I'll give her thanks   185
As though she bid me stay by her a week.
If she deny to wed, I'll crave the day
When I shall ask the banns, and when be marrièd.
But here she comes—and now, Petruchio, speak.

Enter Katherine

Good morrow, Kate, for that's your name, I hear.   190
KATHERINE
Well have you heard, but something hard of hearing.
They call me Katherine that do talk of me.
PETRUCHIO
You lie, in faith, for you are called plain Kate,
And bonny Kate, and sometimes Kate the curst.
But Kate, the prettiest Kate in Christendom,   195
Kate of Kate Hall, my super-dainty Kate
(For dainties are all Kates)—and therefore, Kate,
Take this of me, Kate of my consolation:
Hearing thy mildness praised in every town,
Thy virtues spoke of, and thy beauty sounded   200
(Yet not so deeply as to thee belongs),
Myself am moved to woo thee for my wife.
KATHERINE
"Moved," in good time! Let him that moved you
  hither

87

206. **movable:** (1) piece of furniture; (2) whimsical person

208. **joint stool:** stool made of parts joined or fitted together

211. **bear:** (1) bear children; (2) bear the weight of a man in sexual intercourse

212. **jade:** worthless horse that lacks endurance

214. **light:** Since Petruchio is interrupted, it is impossible to say which of the many meanings of **light** might apply here.

215. **light:** quick; **swain:** rustic lover; bumpkin

217. **buzz:** i.e., the sound of a bee, the **be** of **should be**

218. **ta'en:** taken or understood (sarcastic)

219. **buzzard:** (1) a buzzing insect; (2) a stupid person

220. **turtle:** turtle dove, symbolic of love; **buzzard:** a bird of prey; **take:** (1) capture; (2) mistake

Remove you hence. I knew you at the first   205
You were a movable.

PETRUCHIO
Why, what's a movable?

KATHERINE   A joint stool.

PETRUCHIO
Thou hast hit it. Come, sit on me.

KATHERINE
Asses are made to bear, and so are you.   210

PETRUCHIO
Women are made to bear, and so are you.

KATHERINE
No such jade as you, if me you mean.

PETRUCHIO
Alas, good Kate, I will not burden thee,
For knowing thee to be but young and light—

KATHERINE
Too light for such a swain as you to catch,   215
And yet as heavy as my weight should be.

PETRUCHIO
"Should be"—should buzz!

KATHERINE   Well ta'en, and like a
    buzzard.

PETRUCHIO
O slow-winged turtle, shall a buzzard take thee?   220

KATHERINE
Ay, for a turtle, as he takes a buzzard.

PETRUCHIO
Come, come, you wasp! I' faith, you are too angry.

KATHERINE
If I be waspish, best beware my sting.

PETRUCHIO
My remedy is then to pluck it out.

KATHERINE
Ay, if the fool could find it where it lies.   225

233. **try:** test

237. **arms:** i.e., coat of arms, the mark of a gentleman

238. **herald:** the officer who determined who had the right to bear arms; **in thy books:** in your herald's books; in your good books, i.e., in your favor

239. **crest:** (1) a figure worn atop a knight's helmet; (2) the comb on a rooster or cock; **coxcomb:** fool's cap (See page 94.)

241. **craven:** coward; a defeated cock

243. **crab:** (1) crab apple; (2) sour-faced person

247. **glass:** mirror

249. **aimed:** guessed; **of:** i.e., by

A helmet with a crest. (2.1.239)
From Bonaventura Pistofilo,
Il torneo . . . (1627).

PETRUCHIO
Who knows not where a wasp does wear his sting?
In his tail.
KATHERINE   In his tongue.
PETRUCHIO   Whose tongue?
KATHERINE
Yours, if you talk of tales, and so farewell.   230
PETRUCHIO   What, with my tongue in your tail?
Nay, come again, good Kate. I am a gentleman—
KATHERINE   That I'll try.   *She strikes him.*
PETRUCHIO
I swear I'll cuff you if you strike again.
KATHERINE   So may you lose your arms.   235
If you strike me, you are no gentleman,
And if no gentleman, why then no arms.
PETRUCHIO
A herald, Kate? O, put me in thy books.
KATHERINE   What is your crest? A coxcomb?
PETRUCHIO
A combless cock, so Kate will be my hen.   240
KATHERINE
No cock of mine. You crow too like a craven.
PETRUCHIO
Nay, come, Kate, come. You must not look so sour.
KATHERINE
It is my fashion when I see a crab.
PETRUCHIO
Why, here's no crab, and therefore look not sour.
KATHERINE   There is, there is.   245
PETRUCHIO
Then show it me.
KATHERINE   Had I a glass, I would.
PETRUCHIO   What, you mean my face?
KATHERINE   Well aimed of such a young one.
PETRUCHIO
Now, by Saint George, I am too young for you.   250

254. **sooth:** truth
255. **chafe:** irritate; **tarry:** stay
256. **whit:** bit; **passing:** very
257. **coy:** distant, aloof
258. **a very:** an utter
259. **gamesome:** playful
262. **askance:** aside (in scorn or contempt)
264. **cross:** inclined to oppose or contradict
266. **conference:** conversation
271. **halt:** limp
272. **whom thou keep'st:** i.e., your servants
273. **Dian:** i.e., Diana, the huntress-goddess of chastity
276. **sportful:** lustful
277. **study:** i.e., prepare
278. **mother wit:** natural intelligence

Diana. (2.1.273)
From Robert Whitcombe, *Janua diuorum* . . . (1678).

KATHERINE
  Yet you are withered.
PETRUCHIO   'Tis with cares.
KATHERINE   I care not.
PETRUCHIO
  Nay, hear you, Kate—in sooth, you 'scape not so.
KATHERINE
  I chafe you if I tarry. Let me go.   255
PETRUCHIO
  No, not a whit. I find you passing gentle.
  'Twas told me you were rough, and coy, and sullen,
  And now I find report a very liar.
  For thou art pleasant, gamesome, passing
      courteous,   260
  But slow in speech, yet sweet as springtime flowers.
  Thou canst not frown, thou canst not look askance,
  Nor bite the lip as angry wenches will,
  Nor hast thou pleasure to be cross in talk.
  But thou with mildness entertain'st thy wooers,   265
  With gentle conference, soft, and affable.
  Why does the world report that Kate doth limp?
  O sland'rous world! Kate like the hazel twig
  Is straight, and slender, and as brown in hue
  As hazel nuts, and sweeter than the kernels.   270
  O, let me see thee walk! Thou dost not halt.
KATHERINE
  Go, fool, and whom thou keep'st command.
PETRUCHIO
  Did ever Dian so become a grove
  As Kate this chamber with her princely gait?
  O, be thou Dian and let her be Kate,   275
  And then let Kate be chaste and Dian sportful.
KATHERINE
  Where did you study all this goodly speech?
PETRUCHIO
  It is extempore, from my mother wit.

279. **else:** otherwise

281. **keep you warm:** Proverbial: "He is wise enough that can keep himself warm."

286. **will you, nill you:** i.e., whether you like it or not

287. **for your turn:** just right for you

292. **wild Kate:** pun on "wildcat"

296. **speed:** succeed

300–1. **in your dumps:** depressed, out of sorts

302. **promise:** assure

306. **face:** brazen

A fool wearing a coxcomb. (2.1.239)
From August Redel, *Apophtegmata symbolica* . . . (n.d.).

KATHERINE
  A witty mother, witless else her son.
PETRUCHIO   Am I not wise?   280
KATHERINE   Yes, keep you warm.
PETRUCHIO
  Marry, so I mean, sweet Katherine, in thy bed.
  And therefore, setting all this chat aside,
  Thus in plain terms: your father hath consented
  That you shall be my wife, your dowry 'greed on,   285
  And, will you, nill you, I will marry you.
  Now, Kate, I am a husband for your turn,
  For by this light, whereby I see thy beauty,
  Thy beauty that doth make me like thee well,
  Thou must be married to no man but me.   290
  For I am he am born to tame you, Kate,
  And bring you from a wild Kate to a Kate
  Conformable as other household Kates.

  Enter Baptista, Gremio, ⌈and⌉ Tranio ⌈as Lucentio.⌉

  Here comes your father. Never make denial.
  I must and will have Katherine to my wife.   295
BAPTISTA
  Now, Signior Petruchio, how speed you with my
      daughter?
PETRUCHIO   How but well, sir? How but well?
  It were impossible I should speed amiss.
BAPTISTA
  Why, how now, daughter Katherine? In your   300
      dumps?
KATHERINE
  Call you me daughter? Now I promise you
  You have showed a tender fatherly regard,
  To wish me wed to one half lunatic,
  A madcap ruffian and a swearing Jack,   305
  That thinks with oaths to face the matter out.

95

309. **curst:** quarrelsome, ill-tempered

310. **froward:** strong-willed

311. **hot:** angry

312. **Grissel:** Griselda, the legendary wife who, with superhuman patience, remained obedient and faithful to a cruel husband (Her story is told by Chaucer in *The Clerk's Tale.*)

313. **Lucrece:** After being raped by Tarquin, she committed suicide. (Shakespeare tells her story in *The Rape of Lucrece.*)

319. **speeding:** success

320. **goodnight our part:** i.e., we'll say good-bye to our suits to Bianca

323. **bargained:** agreed; **'twixt:** between

324. **still:** always

328. **vied:** repeated, piled up

329. **twink:** i.e., twinkling of an eye

332. **meacock:** meek

334. **'gainst:** in preparation for

335. **bid:** invite

336. **fine:** splendidly dressed

PETRUCHIO
  Father, 'tis thus: yourself and all the world
  That talked of her have talked amiss of her.
  If she be curst, it is for policy,
  For she's not froward, but modest as the dove;   310
  She is not hot, but temperate as the morn.
  For patience she will prove a second Grissel,
  And Roman Lucrece for her chastity.
  And to conclude, we have 'greed so well together
  That upon Sunday is the wedding day.   315
KATHERINE
  I'll see thee hanged on Sunday first.
GREMIO Hark, Petruchio, she says she'll see thee
  hanged first.
TRANIO, ⌐*as* LUCENTIO⌐ Is this your speeding? Nay,
  then, goodnight our part.   320
PETRUCHIO
  Be patient, gentlemen. I choose her for myself.
  If she and I be pleased, what's that to you?
  'Tis bargained 'twixt us twain, being alone,
  That she shall still be curst in company.
  I tell you, 'tis incredible to believe   325
  How much she loves me. O, the kindest Kate!
  She hung about my neck, and kiss on kiss
  She vied so fast, protesting oath on oath,
  That in a twink she won me to her love.
  O, you are novices! 'Tis a world to see   330
  How tame, when men and women are alone,
  A meacock wretch can make the curstest shrew.—
  Give me thy hand, Kate. I will unto Venice
  To buy apparel 'gainst the wedding day.—
  Provide the feast, father, and bid the guests.   335
  I will be sure my Katherine shall be fine.
BAPTISTA
  I know not what to say, but give me your hands.
  God send you joy, Petruchio. 'Tis a match.

341. **apace:** quickly

344. **clapped up:** hurriedly arranged

345-48. **Faith, gentlemen . . . the seas:** In these lines Baptista compares himself—and is compared —to a merchant who takes a great gamble to dispose of goods (Katherine) which are wearing out from being long kept in storage. **desperate mart:** risky market **commodity:** goods **fretting:** (1) wearing out (of goods); (2) irritable (of Katherine)

350. **he:** i.e., Petruchio

359. **Skipper:** i.e., one young enough that he can skip (term of contempt)

GREMIO and TRANIO, ⌜*as* LUCENTIO⌝
  Amen, say we. We will be witnesses.
PETRUCHIO
  Father, and wife, and gentlemen, adieu.   340
  I will to Venice. Sunday comes apace.
  We will have rings, and things, and fine array,
  And kiss me, Kate. We will be married o' Sunday.
                    Petruchio and Katherine exit
                    ⌜*through different doors.*⌝
GREMIO
  Was ever match clapped up so suddenly?
BAPTISTA
  Faith, gentlemen, now I play a merchant's part   345
  And venture madly on a desperate mart.
TRANIO, ⌜*as* LUCENTIO⌝
  'Twas a commodity lay fretting by you.
  'Twill bring you gain, or perish on the seas.
BAPTISTA
  The gain I seek, is quiet ⌜in⌝ the match.
GREMIO
  No doubt but he hath got a quiet catch.   350
  But now, Baptista, to your younger daughter.
  Now is the day we long have looked for.
  I am your neighbor and was suitor first.
TRANIO, ⌜*as* LUCENTIO⌝
  And I am one that love Bianca more
  Than words can witness or your thoughts can guess.   355
GREMIO
  Youngling, thou canst not love so dear as I.
TRANIO, ⌜*as* LUCENTIO⌝
  Graybeard, thy love doth freeze.
GREMIO   But thine doth fry!
  Skipper, stand back. 'Tis age that nourisheth.
TRANIO, ⌜*as* LUCENTIO⌝
  But youth in ladies' eyes that flourisheth.   360

361. **compound:** settle, reconcile

362. **he of both:** i.e., the one of you two

368. **lave:** wash

369. **hangings:** i.e., wall hangings; **Tyrian:** purple

370. **crowns:** gold coins

371. **arras counterpoints:** counterpanes of Arras tapestry

372. **tents:** perhaps, bed-curtains

373. **Turkey:** Turkish; **bossed:** i.e., embossed

374. **Valance:** drapery; **gold:** i.e., gold thread

377. **milch-kine to the pail:** cows providing milk

378. **Six score:** one hundred twenty

379. **answerable to:** i.e., consistent with; **portion:** estate

380. **struck in years:** stricken with age

383. **list:** listen

390. **ducats:** gold coins; **by the:** per

391. **Of:** from; **fruitful:** fertile; **jointure:** estate, which she will inherit at his death

392. **pinched you:** put you in a tight spot

BAPTISTA
   Content you, gentlemen. I will compound this strife.
   'Tis deeds must win the prize, and he of both
   That can assure my daughter greatest dower
   Shall have my Bianca's love.
   Say, Signior Gremio, what can you assure her?   365
GREMIO
   First, as you know, my house within the city
   Is richly furnishèd with plate and gold,
   Basins and ewers to lave her dainty hands;
   My hangings all of Tyrian tapestry;
   In ivory coffers I have stuffed my crowns,   370
   In cypress chests my arras counterpoints,
   Costly apparel, tents, and canopies,
   Fine linen, Turkey cushions bossed with pearl,
   Valance of Venice gold in needlework,
   Pewter and brass, and all things that belongs   375
   To house or housekeeping. Then, at my farm
   I have a hundred milch-kine to the pail,
   Six score fat oxen standing in my stalls,
   And all things answerable to this portion.
   Myself am struck in years, I must confess,   380
   And if I die tomorrow this is hers,
   If whilst I live she will be only mine.
TRANIO, ⌜*as* LUCENTIO⌝
   That "only" came well in. ⌜*To Baptista.*⌝ Sir, list to
     me:
   I am my father's heir and only son.   385
   If I may have your daughter to my wife,
   I'll leave her houses three or four as good,
   Within rich Pisa walls, as any one
   Old Signior Gremio has in Padua,
   Besides two thousand ducats by the year   390
   Of fruitful land, all which shall be her jointure.—
   What, have I pinched you, Signior Gremio?

395. **argosy:** largest of trading ships

396. **Marcellus' road:** sheltered anchorage outside the harbor at Marseilles

399. **galliasses:** large galleys

400. **tight:** watertight, sound; **assure:** promise

407. **outvied:** outbid

409. **let . . . assurance:** i.e., if your father provides her the guarantee

412. **cavil:** meaningless objection

An argosy. (2.1.395)
From Robert Hitchcock, *A pollitique platt* . . . (1580).

GREMIO
    Two thousand ducats by the year of land?
    ⌜*Aside.*⌝ My land amounts not to so much in all.—
    That she shall have, besides an argosy   395
    That now is lying in Marcellus' road.
    ⌜*To Tranio.*⌝ What, have I choked you with an argosy?
TRANIO, ⌜*as* LUCENTIO⌝
    Gremio, 'tis known my father hath no less
    Than three great argosies, besides two galliasses
    And twelve tight galleys. These I will assure her,   400
    And twice as much whate'er thou off'rest next.
GREMIO
    Nay, I have offered all. I have no more,
    And she can have no more than all I have.
    ⌜*To Baptista.*⌝ If you like me, she shall have me and
        mine.   405
TRANIO, ⌜*as* LUCENTIO⌝
    Why, then, the maid is mine from all the world,
    By your firm promise. Gremio is outvied.
BAPTISTA
    I must confess your offer is the best,
    And, let your father make her the assurance,
    She is your own; else, you must pardon me.   410
    If you should die before him, where's her dower?
TRANIO, ⌜*as* LUCENTIO⌝
    That's but a cavil. He is old, I young.
GREMIO
    And may not young men die as well as old?
BAPTISTA
    Well, gentlemen, I am thus resolved:
    On Sunday next, you know   415
    My daughter Katherine is to be married.
    ⌜*To Tranio as Lucentio.*⌝ Now, on the Sunday
        following, shall Bianca
    Be bride to you, if you make this assurance.
    If not, to Signior Gremio.   420
    And so I take my leave, and thank you both.

424. gamester: gambler, betting on his father's generosity; **were:** i.e., would be

426. Set foot under thy table: i.e., be reduced to a guest in your house; **toy:** joke

428. A vengeance on: i.e., may I be avenged on

429. faced . . . ten: i.e., bluffed it without even a face card

434. get: i.e., beget

435. sire: father; **of:** i.e., in

A galley. (2.1.400)
From Bartolomeo Crescentio, *Nautica Mediterranea* . . . (1607).

GREMIO
　Adieu, good neighbor.　　　　　　⌜*Baptista*⌝ *exits.*
　　　　　　　　　Now I fear thee not.
　Sirrah young gamester, your father were a fool
　To give thee all and in his waning age　　　　　425
　Set foot under thy table. Tut, a toy!
　An old Italian fox is not so kind, my boy.
　　　　　　　　　　　⌜*Gremio*⌝ *exits.*

TRANIO
　A vengeance on your crafty withered hide!—
　Yet I have faced it with a card of ten.
　'Tis in my head to do my master good.　　　　430
　I see no reason but supposed Lucentio
　Must get a father, called "supposed Vincentio"—
　And that's a wonder. Fathers commonly
　Do get their children. But in this case of wooing,
　A child shall get a sire, if I fail not of my cunning.　435
　　　　　　　　　　　　　　He exits.

THE
TAMING
OF THE
SHREW

ACT 3

3.1 Under cover of their disguises as schoolmasters, first Lucentio (as Cambio) and then Hortensio (as Litio) try for Bianca's love. Hortensio notices Lucentio-Cambio's affection for Bianca and determines to abandon her if she shows any interest in such a social inferior as Hortensio believes Cambio to be.

---

1. **forbear:** stop
3. **withal:** i.e., with
4. **this:** i.e., Bianca
6. **leave:** permission; **to have prerogative:** i.e., to go first
8. **Your lecture . . . much:** i.e., your lesson will be given equal time
9. **Preposterous:** literally, putting first what belongs last (Music is to follow work, not precede it.)
10. **ordained:** instituted, created
12. **usual pain:** i.e., daily labor
14. **serve in:** i.e., perform, present
15. **bear these braves:** endure these taunts
18. **breeching scholar:** young student liable to be breeched (i.e., whipped)
19. **'pointed:** i.e., appointed

⌐ACT 3⌐

⌐Scene 1⌐

Enter Lucentio ⌐*as Cambio,*⌐ *Hortensio* ⌐*as Litio,*⌐ *and Bianca.*

LUCENTIO, ⌐*as* CAMBIO⌐
Fiddler, forbear. You grow too forward, sir.
Have you so soon forgot the entertainment
Her sister Katherine welcomed you withal?

HORTENSIO, ⌐*as* LITIO⌐   But, wrangling pedant, this is
The patroness of heavenly harmony.   5
Then give me leave to have prerogative,
And when in music we have spent an hour,
Your lecture shall have leisure for as much.

LUCENTIO, ⌐*as* CAMBIO⌐
Preposterous ass, that never read so far
To know the cause why music was ordained.   10
Was it not to refresh the mind of man
After his studies or his usual pain?
Then give me leave to read philosophy,
And, while I pause, serve in your harmony.

HORTENSIO, ⌐*as* LITIO⌐
Sirrah, I will not bear these braves of thine.   15

BIANCA
Why, gentlemen, you do me double wrong
To strive for that which resteth in my choice.
I am no breeching scholar in the schools.
I'll not be tied to hours, nor 'pointed times,

109

30–31. Hic . . . senis: "Here flowed the Simois; here is the Sigeian land; / Here had stood old Priam's high palace" (Ovid).

32. Conster: construe, interpret

35. thus: i.e., as the tutor Cambio

37. bearing my port: assuming my social position

38. pantaloon: i.e., Gremio (see note to 1.1.45 SD)

41. jars: is out of tune

42–43. Spit . . . again: an ironic twist on the proverbial "Spit on your hands and try again"

50. base knave: i.e., "Cambio"

But learn my lessons as I please myself.   20
And, to cut off all strife, here sit we down.
⌐To Hortensio.⌐ Take you your instrument, play you
    the whiles;
His lecture will be done ere you have tuned.
HORTENSIO, ⌐as LITIO⌐
You'll leave his lecture when I am in tune?   25
LUCENTIO, ⌐aside⌐
That will be never. ⌐To Hortensio.⌐ Tune your
    instrument. ⌐Hortensio steps aside to tune his lute.⌐
BIANCA   Where left we last?
LUCENTIO, ⌐as CAMBIO⌐ Here, madam:
                            ⌐Showing her a book.⌐
Hic ibat Simois, hic est ⌐Sigeia⌐ tellus,   30
Hic steterat Priami regia celsa senis.
BIANCA   Conster them.
LUCENTIO   Hic ibat, as I told you before, Simois, I am
    Lucentio, hic est, son unto Vincentio of Pisa,
    ⌐Sigeia⌐ tellus, disguised thus to get your love, Hic   35
    steterat, and that "Lucentio" that comes a-wooing,
    Priami, is my man Tranio, regia, bearing my port,
    celsa senis, that we might beguile the old pantaloon.
HORTENSIO, ⌐as LITIO⌐ Madam, my instrument's in
    tune.   40
BIANCA   Let's hear. ⌐He plays.⌐ Oh fie, the treble jars!
LUCENTIO, ⌐as CAMBIO⌐ Spit in the hole, man, and tune
    again.   ⌐Hortensio tunes his lute again.⌐
BIANCA   Now let me see if I can conster it. Hic ibat
    Simois, I know you not; hic est ⌐Sigeia⌐ tellus, I trust 45
    you not; Hic ⌐steterat⌐ Priami, take heed he hear us
    not; regia, presume not; celsa senis, despair not.
HORTENSIO, ⌐as LITIO⌐
Madam, 'tis now in tune.   ⌐He plays again.⌐
LUCENTIO, ⌐as CAMBIO⌐   All but the bass.
HORTENSIO, ⌐as LITIO⌐
The bass is right. 'Tis the base knave that jars.   50

111

53. **Pedascule:** corrupt Latin for "little pedant" (pronounced with four syllables)

55. **Aeacides:** Lucentio is pretending to interpret Ovid to Bianca. The reference to **Aeacides** ("descendant of Aeacus") follows in Ovid the passage quoted at lines 30–31.

61. **pleasant:** merry

62. **give me leave:** let me alone

65. **withal:** as well; **but:** unless

68. **learn:** i.e., teach; **order:** system

70. **gamut:** the musical scale devised in the 11th century. The notes—known as A, B, C, etc.—were sung to the syllables *re, mi, fa, sol, la,* and *ut* (see lines 76–81). The "gamut" was also the ground note of the scale.

73. **drawn:** set out

⌐*Aside.*⌐ How fiery and forward our pedant is.
Now for my life the knave doth court my love!
Pedascule, I'll watch you better yet.
⌐BIANCA, *to Lucentio*⌐
In time I may believe, yet I mistrust.
⌐LUCENTIO⌐
Mistrust it not, for sure Aeacides   55
Was Ajax, called so from his grandfather.
⌐BIANCA⌐
I must believe my master; else, I promise you,
I should be arguing still upon that doubt.
But let it rest.—Now, Litio, to you.
Good master, take it not unkindly, pray,   60
That I have been thus pleasant with you both.
HORTENSIO, ⌐*as* LITIO, *to Lucentio*⌐
You may go walk, and give me leave awhile.
My lessons make no music in three parts.
LUCENTIO, ⌐*as* CAMBIO⌐
Are you so formal, sir? Well, I must wait
⌐*Aside.*⌐ And watch withal, for, but I be deceived,   65
Our fine musician groweth amorous.
                    ⌐*He steps aside.*⌐
HORTENSIO, ⌐*as* LITIO⌐
Madam, before you touch the instrument,
To learn the order of my fingering
I must begin with rudiments of art,
To teach you gamut in a briefer sort,   70
More pleasant, pithy, and effectual
Than hath been taught by any of my trade.
And there it is in writing fairly drawn.
BIANCA
Why, I am past my gamut long ago.
HORTENSIO
Yet read the gamut of Hortensio.   75
                    ⌐*Giving her a paper.*⌐

83. **nice:** hard to please
84. **To:** i.e., so as to
91. **Methinks:** I think
92. **humble:** common, low, base
93. **stale:** decoy, lure (term from falconry)
94–95. **Seize . . . changing:** i.e., Let anyone who wants you capture you. If I once find you untrue, I will get even with you by turning to someone else.

3.2 Petruchio is late arriving for his wedding, to Katherine's great embarrassment. When he finally presents himself, he is dressed in ridiculous clothes. At the wedding, according to Gremio's report, Petruchio behaves rudely and abusively. He refuses to attend the supper that traditionally follows a wedding, and he insists on taking Katherine away as well. Over her protests, he forces her to go with him, making a show of defending her against the interference of her family and friends.

1. **'pointed:** i.e., appointed

BIANCA ⌈*reads*⌉
    "*Gamut* I am, the ground of all accord:
    ⌈*A re,*⌉ to plead Hortensio's passion;
    ⌈*B mi,*⌉ Bianca, take him for thy lord,
    ⌈*C fa ut,*⌉ that loves with all affection;
    D sol re, one clef, two notes have I;   80
    E la mi, show pity or I die."
    Call you this "gamut"? Tut, I like it not.
    Old fashions please me best. I am not so nice
    To ⌈change⌉ true rules for ⌈odd⌉ inventions.
                    Enter a ⌈*Servant.*⌉

⌈SERVANT⌉
    Mistress, your father prays you leave your books   85
    And help to dress your sister's chamber up.
    You know tomorrow is the wedding day.
BIANCA
    Farewell, sweet masters both. I must be gone.
LUCENTIO
    Faith, mistress, then I have no cause to stay.
                    ⌈*Bianca, the Servant, and Lucentio exit.*⌉
HORTENSIO
    But I have cause to pry into this pedant.   90
    Methinks he looks as though he were in love.
    Yet if thy thoughts, Bianca, be so humble
    To cast thy wand'ring eyes on every stale,
    Seize thee that list! If once I find thee ranging,
    Hortensio will be quit with thee by changing.   95
                    He exits.

                    ⌈Scene 2⌉
Enter Baptista, Gremio, Tranio ⌈*as Lucentio,*⌉ *Katherine,*
Bianca, ⌈*Lucentio as Cambio,*⌉ *and others, Attendants.*

BAPTISTA, ⌈*to Tranio*⌉
    Signior Lucentio, this is the 'pointed day

                    115

5. **want:** lack; **attends:** awaits; is present
8. **forsooth:** indeed
10. **rudesby:** rude, disorderly fellow; **spleen:** impulsiveness, changeableness
12. **frantic:** lunatic, insane
13. **blunt:** rude
14. **noted for:** known as
16. **proclaim the banns:** announce the intended marriage
22. **means but:** only means
23. **Whatever . . . word:** whatever accident prevents him from keeping his promise to be married
24. **passing:** very
27. **to weep:** i.e., for weeping
29. **humor:** temperament

That Katherine and Petruchio should be married,
And yet we hear not of our son-in-law.
What will be said? What mockery will it be,
To want the bridegroom when the priest attends   5
To speak the ceremonial rites of marriage?
What says Lucentio to this shame of ours?

KATHERINE
No shame but mine. I must, forsooth, be forced
To give my hand, opposed against my heart,
Unto a mad-brain rudesby, full of spleen,   10
Who wooed in haste and means to wed at leisure.
I told you, I, he was a frantic fool,
Hiding his bitter jests in blunt behavior,
And, to be noted for a merry man,
He'll woo a thousand, 'point the day of marriage,   15
Make friends, invite, and proclaim the banns,
Yet never means to wed where he hath wooed.
Now must the world point at poor Katherine
And say "Lo, there is mad Petruchio's wife,
If it would please him come and marry her."   20

TRANIO, ⌐as LUCENTIO⌐
Patience, good Katherine, and Baptista too.
Upon my life, Petruchio means but well,
Whatever fortune stays him from his word.
Though he be blunt, I know him passing wise;
Though he be merry, yet withal he's honest.   25

KATHERINE
Would Katherine had never seen him, though!
                              She exits weeping.

BAPTISTA
Go, girl. I cannot blame thee now to weep,
For such an injury would vex a very saint,
Much more a shrew of ⌐thy⌐ impatient humor.

                    Enter Biondello.

BIONDELLO   Master, master, news! And such ⌐old⌐   30
news as you never heard of!

117

41. **to:** i.e., about

43. **jerkin:** short jacket; **turned:** i.e., turned inside out in order to get more wear out of them

44. **candle-cases:** i.e., used as places to throw candle ends

47. **chapeless:** without the metal plate (**chape**) on its sheath; **points:** laces to hold up stockings

48. **hipped:** lame in the hip

48–49. **of no kindred:** i.e., that do not match

49. **glanders:** swelling glands and nasal discharge

50. **like . . . chine:** possibly, likely to decay in the backbone; or possibly, susceptible to glanders

50–51. **lampass:** swelling in the mouth

51. **fashions:** i.e., farcins, a disease in horses causing painful ulcerations, especially on the legs; **windgalls:** tumors on its legs

52. **sped with spavins:** ruined by inflamed cartilage; **rayed with the yellows:** berayed or disfigured by jaundice

53. **fives:** avives, a disease causing swelling below the ears; **stark:** entirely; **the staggers:** staggering, giddiness; **begnawn:** gnawed; eaten away

54. **bots:** intestinal worms

54–55. **shoulder-shotten:** lame in the shoulder

55. **near-legged before:** with knock-kneed forelegs

55–56. **half-checked bit:** i.e., a faulty bit

56. **headstall:** part of the bridle; **sheep's leather:** i.e., inferior leather, not the preferable pigskin

59. **pieced:** repaired

60. **crupper:** the strap under the horse's tail that keeps the saddle steady; **velour:** velvet (thus less sturdy than a leather crupper)

62. **pieced . . . thread:** held together with string

BAPTISTA
  Is it new and old too? How may that be?
BIONDELLO   Why, is it not news to ⌜hear⌝ of Petruchio's
  coming?
BAPTISTA   Is he come?   35
BIONDELLO   Why, no, sir.
BAPTISTA
  What then?
BIONDELLO   He is coming.
BAPTISTA   When will he be here?
BIONDELLO
  When he stands where I am, and sees you there.   40
TRANIO, ⌜as LUCENTIO⌝   But say, what to thine old news?
BIONDELLO   Why, Petruchio is coming in a new hat and
  an old jerkin, a pair of old breeches thrice turned,
  a pair of boots that have been candle-cases, one
  buckled, another laced; an old rusty sword ta'en   45
  out of the town armory, with a broken hilt, and
  chapeless; with two broken points; his horse
  hipped, with an old mothy saddle and stirrups of no
  kindred, besides possessed with the glanders and
  like to mose in the chine, troubled with the lam-   50
  pass, infected with the fashions, full of windgalls,
  sped with spavins, rayed with the yellows, past cure
  of the fives, stark spoiled with the staggers, begnawn
  with the bots, ⌜swayed⌝ in the back and shoulder-
  shotten, near-legged before, and with a half-   55
  checked bit and a headstall of sheep's leather,
  which, being restrained to keep him from stum-
  bling, hath been often burst, and now repaired with
  knots; one girth six times pieced, and a woman's
  crupper of velour, which hath two letters for her   60
  name fairly set down in studs, and here and there
  pieced with packthread.
BAPTISTA   Who comes with him?

64–65. **caparisoned:** outfitted
65. **stock:** stocking
66. **kersey boot-hose:** coarse wool stocking
67. **list:** cloth border
67–68. **humor . . . in 't:** perhaps, decorated in a wildly extravagant way
69. **monster:** beast that combines several forms
71. **humor:** whim, mood; **pricks:** urges
72. **mean-appareled:** dressed poorly
80. **all one:** i.e., the same thing
82. **hold:** bet
86. **gallants:** fine gentlemen
89. **halt:** limp

BIONDELLO Oh, sir, his lackey, for all the world caparisoned like the horse: with a linen stock on one leg   65
and a kersey boot-hose on the other, gartered with
a red and blue list; an old hat, and the humor of
forty fancies pricked in 't for a feather. A monster,
a very monster in apparel, and not like a Christian
footboy or a gentleman's lackey.   70

TRANIO, ⌈as LUCENTIO⌉
'Tis some odd humor pricks him to this fashion,
Yet oftentimes he goes but mean-appareled.

BAPTISTA
I am glad he's come, howsoe'er he comes.

BIONDELLO Why, sir, he comes not.

BAPTISTA Didst thou not say he comes?   75

BIONDELLO Who? That Petruchio came?

BAPTISTA Ay, that Petruchio came!

BIONDELLO No, sir, I say his horse comes with him on
his back.

BAPTISTA Why, that's all one.   80

BIONDELLO

> Nay, by Saint Jamy.
> I hold you a penny,
> A horse and a man
> Is more than one,
> And yet not many.   85

Enter Petruchio and Grumio.

PETRUCHIO
Come, where be these gallants? Who's at home?

BAPTISTA You are welcome, sir.

PETRUCHIO And yet I come not well.

BAPTISTA And yet you halt not.

TRANIO, ⌈as LUCENTIO⌉ Not so well appareled as I wish   90
you were.

PETRUCHIO
Were it better I should rush in thus—

94. **Gentles:** i.e., gentlemen
95. **wherefore:** why
97. **prodigy:** wonder
100. **unprovided:** unprepared
101. **this habit:** these clothes; **estate:** status
102. **solemn:** ceremonial
103. **import:** importance
108. **in some part:** to some extent; **enforcèd to digress:** forced to deviate (from his promise)
113. **unreverent:** unrespectable
117. **Good sooth:** in truth
121. **accoutrements:** clothes

But where is Kate? Where is my lovely bride?
How does my father? Gentles, methinks you frown.
And wherefore gaze this goodly company   95
As if they saw some wondrous monument,
Some comet or unusual prodigy?
BAPTISTA
Why, sir, you know this is your wedding day.
First were we sad, fearing you would not come,
Now sadder that you come so unprovided.   100
Fie, doff this habit, shame to your estate,
An eyesore to our solemn festival.
TRANIO, ⌜as LUCENTIO⌝
And tell us what occasion of import
Hath all so long detainèd you from your wife
And sent you hither so unlike yourself.   105
PETRUCHIO
Tedious it were to tell, and harsh to hear.
Sufficeth I am come to keep my word,
Though in some part enforcèd to digress,
Which at more leisure I will so excuse
As you shall well be satisfied with all.   110
But where is Kate? I stay too long from her.
The morning wears. 'Tis time we were at church.
TRANIO, ⌜as LUCENTIO⌝
See not your bride in these unreverent robes.
Go to my chamber, put on clothes of mine.
PETRUCHIO
Not I, believe me. Thus I'll visit her.   115
BAPTISTA
But thus, I trust, you will not marry her.
PETRUCHIO
Good sooth, even thus. Therefore, ha' done with
    words.
To me she's married, not unto my clothes.
Could I repair what she will wear in me,   120
As I can change these poor accoutrements,

125. **seal:** i.e., ratify; **lovely:** i.e., loving
127. **be it:** i.e., if it be
129. **event:** outcome
130. **love:** i.e., Bianca's love (The abruptness of the change of subject may reflect some lost lines of text. It has been suggested that Tranio and Lucentio should enter at this point, and that the lines earlier in the scene given to Tranio should, in fact, be given to Hortensio, for whom they are much more appropriate.)
134. **skills:** i.e., matters; **turn:** purpose
136. **make assurance:** provide guarantees
141. **narrowly:** closely
142. **steal our marriage:** i.e., elope (**marriage** pronounced as a three-syllable word)
145. **That:** i.e., the marriage; **by degrees:** gradually
146. **watch our vantage:** look out for opportunities that favor us
148. **narrow prying:** i.e., overly watchful
149. **quaint:** cunning, crafty

'Twere well for Kate and better for myself.
But what a fool am I to chat with you
When I should bid good morrow to my bride
And seal the title with a lovely kiss!   125
          Petruchio exits, ⌐*with Grumio.*⌐

TRANIO, ⌐*as* LUCENTIO⌐
He hath some meaning in his mad attire.
We will persuade him, be it possible,
To put on better ere he go to church.

BAPTISTA
I'll after him, and see the event of this.
        ⌐*All except Tranio and Lucentio*⌐ *exit.*

TRANIO
But, sir, ⌐to⌐ love concerneth us to add   130
Her father's liking, which to bring to pass,
As ⌐I⌐ before imparted to your Worship,
I am to get a man (whate'er he be
It skills not much, we'll fit him to our turn),
And he shall be "Vincentio of Pisa,"   135
And make assurance here in Padua
Of greater sums than I have promisèd.
So shall you quietly enjoy your hope
And marry sweet Bianca with consent.

LUCENTIO
Were it not that my fellow schoolmaster   140
Doth watch Bianca's steps so narrowly,
'Twere good, methinks, to steal our marriage,
Which, once performed, let all the world say no,
I'll keep mine own despite of all the world.

TRANIO
That by degrees we mean to look into,   145
And watch our vantage in this business.
We'll overreach the graybeard, Gremio,
The narrow prying father, Minola,
The quaint musician, amorous Litio,
All for my master's sake, Lucentio.   150

156. **Curster:** more perverse
158. **dam:** mother
159. **fool:** pitiable creature
161. **Should ask:** i.e., asked; **should:** would
162. **gog's wouns:** i.e., God's wounds (a strong oath)
163. **amazed:** astounded
165. **took:** hit
167. **he:** i.e., Petruchio; **list:** wishes to
169. **for why:** because
170. **vicar:** priest; **cozen:** cheat
172. **health:** toast
173. **aboard:** i.e., on shipboard
174. **quaffed:** drank

Enter Gremio.

TRANIO, ⌜*as* LUCENTIO⌝
Signior Gremio, came you from the church?
GREMIO
As willingly as e'er I came from school.
TRANIO, ⌜*as* LUCENTIO⌝
And is the bride and bridegroom coming home?
GREMIO
A bridegroom, say you? 'Tis a groom indeed,
A grumbling groom, and that the girl shall find.   155
TRANIO, ⌜*as* LUCENTIO⌝
Curster than she? Why, 'tis impossible.
GREMIO
Why, he's a devil, a devil, a very fiend.
TRANIO, ⌜*as* LUCENTIO⌝
Why, she's a devil, a devil, the devil's dam.
GREMIO
Tut, she's a lamb, a dove, a fool to him.
I'll tell you, Sir Lucentio: when the priest   160
Should ask if Katherine should be his wife,
"Ay, by gog's wouns!" quoth he, and swore so loud
That, all amazed, the priest let fall the book,
And as he stooped again to take it up,
This mad-brained bridegroom took him such a cuff   165
That down fell priest and book, and book and priest.
"Now, take them up," quoth he, "if any list."
TRANIO, ⌜*as* LUCENTIO⌝
What said the wench when he rose again?
GREMIO
Trembled and shook, for why he stamped and swore
As if the vicar meant to cozen him.   170
But after many ceremonies done,
He calls for wine. "A health!" quoth he, as if
He had been aboard, carousing to his mates
After a storm; quaffed off the muscatel

127

175. **sops:** cake that had been broken up and soaked in the wine; **sexton:** church officer

177. **his:** i.e., the sexton's; **hungerly:** sparsely

178. **to ask him sops:** i.e., to require sops

183. **rout:** crowd

185 SD. **Hortensio:** It is unclear whether Hortensio enters here as "Litio" or as himself.

188. **store:** quantities; **cheer:** food and drink

193. **Make it no wonder:** do not wonder at it

198. **my father:** i.e., my father-in-law, Baptista

And threw the sops all in the sexton's face,   175
Having no other reason
But that his beard grew thin and hungerly,
And seemed to ask him sops as he was drinking.
This done, he took the bride about the neck
And kissed her lips with such a clamorous smack   180
That at the parting all the church did echo.
And I, seeing this, came thence for very shame,
And after me I know the rout is coming.
Such a mad marriage never was before! *Music plays.*
Hark, hark, I hear the minstrels play.   185

Enter Petruchio, Katherine, Bianca, Hortensio, Baptista,
⌜*Grumio, and Attendants.*⌝

PETRUCHIO
Gentlemen and friends, I thank you for your pains.
I know you think to dine with me today
And have prepared great store of wedding cheer,
But so it is, my haste doth call me hence,
And therefore here I mean to take my leave.   190
BAPTISTA
Is 't possible you will away tonight?
PETRUCHIO
I must away today, before night come.
Make it no wonder. If you knew my business,
You would entreat me rather go than stay.
And, honest company, I thank you all,   195
That have beheld me give away myself
To this most patient, sweet, and virtuous wife.
Dine with my father, drink a health to me,
For I must hence, and farewell to you all.
TRANIO, ⌜*as* LUCENTIO⌝
Let us entreat you stay till after dinner.   200
PETRUCHIO It may not be.
GREMIO Let me entreat you.
PETRUCHIO It cannot be.

217. **jogging . . . green:** going while your boots are new (an invitation to leave)

219. **like:** i.e., likely; **jolly:** i.e., overbearing

220. **That take . . . roundly:** i.e., in that you immediately presume to take command so completely

222. **What . . . do?:** i.e., what business is it of yours?

223. **stay my leisure:** i.e., wait until I am ready

224. **marry:** i.e., indeed

230. **domineer:** feast riotously (Dutch *domineren*, to feast luxuriously)

KATHERINE   Let me entreat you.
PETRUCHIO
  I am content.   205
KATHERINE   Are you content to stay?
PETRUCHIO
  I am content you shall entreat me stay,
  But yet not stay, entreat me how you can.
KATHERINE
  Now, if you love me, stay.
PETRUCHIO   Grumio, my horse.   210
GRUMIO   Ay, sir, they be ready; the oats have eaten the
    horses.
KATHERINE   Nay, then,
  Do what thou canst, I will not go today,
  No, nor tomorrow, not till I please myself.   215
  The door is open, sir. There lies your way.
  You may be jogging whiles your boots are green.
  For me, I'll not be gone till I please myself.
  'Tis like you'll prove a jolly surly groom,
  That take it on you at the first so roundly.   220
PETRUCHIO
  O Kate, content thee. Prithee, be not angry.
KATHERINE
  I will be angry. What hast thou to do?—
  Father, be quiet. He shall stay my leisure.
GREMIO
  Ay, marry, sir, now it begins to work.
KATHERINE
  Gentlemen, forward to the bridal dinner.   225
  I see a woman may be made a fool
  If she had not a spirit to resist.
PETRUCHIO
  They shall go forward, Kate, at thy command.—
  Obey the bride, you that attend on her.
  Go to the feast, revel and domineer,   230
  Carouse full measure to her maidenhead,

234. **big:** challenging, defiant
236. **chattels:** property, goods
237. **stuff:** goods
240. **bring mine action:** (1) bring legal action; (2) attack physically; **he:** i.e., one
246. **buckler:** i.e., defend
248. **Went they not:** i.e., if they had not gone
251. **mated:** matched, married
254–55. **wants . . . supply:** i.e., are not present to occupy
256. **wants:** are lacking; **junkets:** confections
259. **room:** place

Be mad and merry, or go hang yourselves.
But for my bonny Kate, she must with me.
Nay, look not big, nor stamp, nor stare, nor fret;
I will be master of what is mine own.   235
She is my goods, my chattels; she is my house,
My household stuff, my field, my barn,
My horse, my ox, my ass, my anything.
And here she stands, touch her whoever dare.
I'll bring mine action on the proudest he   240
That stops my way in Padua.—Grumio,
Draw forth thy weapon. We are beset with thieves.
Rescue thy mistress if thou be a man!—
Fear not, sweet wench, they shall not touch thee,
    Kate.   245
I'll buckler thee against a million.
        Petruchio and Katherine exit, ⌜with Grumio.⌝

BAPTISTA
Nay, let them go. A couple of quiet ones!

GREMIO
Went they not quickly, I should die with laughing.

TRANIO, ⌜*as* LUCENTIO⌝
Of all mad matches never was the like.

LUCENTIO, ⌜*as* CAMBIO⌝
Mistress, what's your opinion of your sister?   250

BIANCA
That being mad herself, she's madly mated.

GREMIO
I warrant him, Petruchio is Kated.

BAPTISTA
Neighbors and friends, though bride and
    bridegroom wants
For to supply the places at the table,   255
You know there wants no junkets at the feast.
⌜*To Tranio.*⌝ Lucentio, you shall supply the
    bridegroom's place,
And let Bianca take her sister's room.

TRANIO, ⌜*as* LUCENTIO⌝
    Shall sweet Bianca practice how to bride it?   260
BAPTISTA, ⌜*to Tranio*⌝
    She shall, Lucentio. Come, gentlemen, let's go.
                                                They exit.

THE
TAMING
OF THE
SHREW

ACT 4

4.1 At Petruchio's house in the country, Grumio tells his fellow servant Curtis about the wild journey home to Petruchio's after the wedding. When Petruchio and Katherine arrive, Petruchio attacks his servants verbally and physically. He refuses to let Katherine eat, saying the dinner is burnt and throwing it to the floor. At the end of the scene he confides to the audience that he intends to tame Katherine in the same way that a hunter tames a falcon—by starving it and keeping it sleepless.

---

1. **jades:** worthless horses
2. **foul ways:** dirty roads
3. **'rayed:** i.e., berayed, dirty
6. **hot:** Proverbial: "A small pot is soon hot."

⌜ACT 4⌝

⌜Scene 1⌝
Enter Grumio.

GRUMIO   Fie, fie on all tired jades, on all mad masters,
and all foul ways! Was ever man so beaten? Was
ever man so 'rayed? Was ever man so weary? I am
sent before to make a fire, and they are coming
after to warm them. Now were not I a little pot and   5
soon hot, my very lips might freeze to my teeth, my
tongue to the roof of my mouth, my heart in my
belly, ere I should come by a fire to thaw me. But I
with blowing the fire shall warm myself. For, considering the weather, a taller man than I will take   10
cold.—Holla, ho, Curtis!

Enter Curtis.

CURTIS   Who is that calls so coldly?
GRUMIO   A piece of ice. If thou doubt it, thou mayst
slide from my shoulder to my heel with no greater
a run but my head and my neck. A fire, good Curtis!   15
CURTIS   Is my master and his wife coming, Grumio?
GRUMIO   Oh, ay, Curtis, ay, and therefore fire, fire! Cast
on no water.
CURTIS   Is she so hot a shrew as she's reported?
GRUMIO   She was, good Curtis, before this frost. But   20
thou know'st winter tames man, woman, and

139

24. **three-inch fool:** another reference to Grumio's short stature (compare **little pot**)

25. **horn:** the symbol of the cuckold (the husband whose wife is unfaithful)

27. **on:** i.e., about

28. **at hand:** nearby

30. **office:** duty (of lighting a fire)

34. **have thy duty:** i.e., get what is due to you

39. **"Jack boy, ho boy!":** a line from a song

41. **cony-catching:** deception (Literally, a cony is a rabbit. In **cony-catching**, the cony is the victim of trickery and deception.)

44. **rushes strewed:** i.e., as floor covering.

45. **fustian:** coarse-cloth work-clothes

46. **officer:** household servant

47. **Jacks:** (1) menservants; (2) large leather drinking cups; **Jills:** (1) women servants; (2) small metal drinking cups

48. **carpets:** probably, woolen table covers

beast, for it hath tamed my old master and my new
mistress and myself, fellow Curtis.

⌜CURTIS⌝   Away, you three-inch fool, I am no beast!

⌜GRUMIO⌝   Am I but three inches? Why, thy horn is a   25
foot, and so long am I, at the least. But wilt thou
make a fire? Or shall I complain on thee to our
mistress, whose hand (she being now at hand) thou
shalt soon feel, to thy cold comfort, for being slow in
thy hot office?   30

CURTIS   I prithee, good Grumio, tell me, how goes the
world?

GRUMIO   A cold world, Curtis, in every office but thine,
and therefore fire! Do thy duty, and have thy duty,
for my master and mistress are almost frozen to   35
death.

CURTIS   There's fire ready. And therefore, good Grumio, the news!

GRUMIO   Why, "Jack boy, ho boy!" and as much news
as wilt thou.   40

CURTIS   Come, you are so full of cony-catching.

GRUMIO   Why, therefore fire, for I have caught extreme
cold. Where's the cook? Is supper ready, the house
trimmed, rushes strewed, cobwebs swept, the servingmen in their new fustian, ⌜their⌝ white stock-   45
ings, and every officer his wedding garment on? Be
the Jacks fair within, the Jills fair without, the
carpets laid, and everything in order?

CURTIS   All ready. And therefore, I pray thee, news.

GRUMIO   First, know my horse is tired, my master and   50
mistress fallen out.

CURTIS   How?

GRUMIO   Out of their saddles into the dirt, and thereby
hangs a tale.

CURTIS   Let's ha' t, good Grumio.   55

GRUMIO   Lend thine ear.

CURTIS   Here.

60. **sensible:** (1) making sense; (2) felt by the senses

62. **Imprimis:** Latin for "first"

63. **foul:** dirty

64. **of:** i.e., on

70. **miry:** swampy; **bemoiled:** muddied

74. **that:** i.e., who

78. **unexperienced:** uninformed

79. **reck'ning:** account

81. **what:** i.e., why

84. **blue coats:** servants' uniforms

85. **indifferent:** equal, i.e., matched

92. **to countenance:** to show respect (pun on the meaning "to face" in the next line)

A cony. (4.1.41)
From the title page of Robert Greene, *Notable discouery of coosenage . . . practised by . . . connie-catchers . . .* (1592).

GRUMIO   There!   ⌐*He slaps Curtis on the ear.*⌐
CURTIS   This 'tis to feel a tale, not to hear a tale.
GRUMIO   And therefore 'tis called a sensible tale. And   60
   this cuff was but to knock at your ear and beseech
   list'ning. Now I begin: *Imprimis*, we came down a
   foul hill, my master riding behind my mistress—
CURTIS   Both of one horse?
GRUMIO   What's that to thee?   65
CURTIS   Why, a horse.
GRUMIO   Tell thou the tale! But hadst thou not crossed
   me, thou shouldst have heard how her horse fell,
   and she under her horse; thou shouldst have heard
   in how miry a place, how she was bemoiled, how he   70
   left her with the horse upon her, how he beat me
   because her horse stumbled, how she waded
   through the dirt to pluck him off me, how he swore,
   how she prayed that never prayed before, how I
   cried, how the horses ran away, how her bridle was   75
   burst, how I lost my crupper, with many things of
   worthy memory which now shall die in oblivion,
   and thou return unexperienced to thy grave.
CURTIS   By this reck'ning, he is more shrew than she.
GRUMIO   Ay, and that thou and the proudest of you all   80
   shall find when he comes home. But what talk I of
   this? Call forth Nathaniel, Joseph, Nicholas, Phillip, Walter, Sugarsop, and the rest. Let their heads
   be slickly combed, their blue coats brushed, and
   their garters of an indifferent knit. Let them curtsy   85
   with their left legs, and not presume to touch a hair
   of my master's horse-tail till they kiss their hands.
   Are they all ready?
CURTIS   They are.
GRUMIO   Call them forth.   90
CURTIS, ⌐*calling out*⌐ Do you hear, ho? You must meet
   my master to countenance my mistress.
GRUMIO   Why, she hath a face of her own.

97. **credit her:** pay respect to her (but "lend her money" in the next line)

106. **spruce:** (1) lively; (2) smart in appearance

111. **Cock's:** i.e., God or Christ's

117. **loggerheaded:** blockheaded

121. **swain:** country bumpkin; **whoreson:** literally, son of a whore; a good-for-nothing

121–22. **malt-horse drudge:** stupid slave (literally, a horse on a treadmill that grinds malt in a brewery)

A malt horse. (4.1.121)
From Georg Andreas Böckler,
Theatrum machinarum novum . . . (1662).

CURTIS Who knows not that?

GRUMIO Thou, it seems, that calls for company to   95
countenance her.

CURTIS I call them forth to credit her.

GRUMIO Why, she comes to borrow nothing of them.

Enter four or five Servingmen.

NATHANIEL Welcome home, Grumio.

PHILLIP How now, Grumio?   100

JOSEPH What, Grumio!

NICHOLAS Fellow Grumio!

NATHANIEL How now, old lad?

GRUMIO Welcome, you!—How now, you?—What,
you!—Fellow, you!—And thus much for greeting.   105
Now, my spruce companions, is all ready and all
things neat?

NATHANIEL All things is ready. How near is our master?

⌜GRUMIO⌝ E'en at hand, alighted by this. And therefore   110
be not—Cock's passion, silence! I hear my master.

Enter Petruchio and Katherine.

PETRUCHIO
Where be these knaves? What, no man at door
To hold my stirrup nor to take my horse?
Where is Nathaniel, Gregory, Phillip?

ALL THE SERVANTS Here! Here, sir, here, sir!   115

PETRUCHIO
"Here, sir! Here, sir! Here, sir! Here, sir!"
You loggerheaded and unpolished grooms.
What? No attendance? No regard? No duty?
Where is the foolish knave I sent before?

GRUMIO
Here, sir, as foolish as I was before.   120

PETRUCHIO
You peasant swain, you whoreson malt-horse
drudge!

145

123. **park:** grounds

126. **unpinked:** undecorated (literally, without ornamental holes punched in them)

127. **link:** blacking from a torch

136. **Soud:** No meaning for this word is recorded; it is often changed to "Food" in texts of this play.

139. **When:** i.e., how long do I have to wait

144. **mend . . . other:** do better in removing the other boot

Did I not bid thee meet me in the park
And bring along these rascal knaves with thee?
GRUMIO
Nathaniel's coat, sir, was not fully made,   125
And Gabriel's pumps were all unpinked i' th' heel.
There was no link to color Peter's hat,
And Walter's dagger was not come from sheathing.
There were none fine but Adam, Rafe, and Gregory.
The rest were ragged, old, and beggarly.   130
Yet, as they are, here are they come to meet you.
PETRUCHIO
Go, rascals, go, and fetch my supper in!
                                        The Servants exit.
⌜*Sings.*⌝   *Where is the life that late I led?*
               Where are those—
Sit down, Kate, and welcome.—   135
                              ⌜*They sit at a table.*⌝
Soud, soud, soud, soud!

               Enter Servants with supper.

Why, when, I say?—Nay, good sweet Kate, be
    merry.—
Off with my boots, you rogues, you villains! When?
⌜*Sings.*⌝   *It was the friar of orders gray,*   140
               As he forth walkèd on his way—

          ⌜*Servant begins to remove Petruchio's boots.*⌝

Out, you rogue! You pluck my foot awry.
Take that!   ⌜*He hits the Servant.*⌝
               And mend the plucking of the other.—
Be merry, Kate.—Some water here! What ho!   145

               Enter one with water.

Where's my spaniel Troilus? Sirrah, get you hence
And bid my cousin Ferdinand come hither.
                              ⌜*A Servant exits.*⌝

152. **it:** i.e., the basin of water

153. **unwilling:** involuntary

154. **beetle-headed:** thickheaded (A beetle was a mallet with a heavy head.)

155. **stomach:** appetite

163. **dresser:** sideboard; or, person who prepared it

165. **trenchers:** wooden platters

166. **joltheads:** blockheads

167. **be . . . straight:** deal with you immediately

172. **choler:** one of the four bodily humors. (Excess choler made one angry.)

175. **it:** i.e., our predisposition to anger

One, Kate, that you must kiss and be acquainted
   with.—
Where are my slippers? Shall I have some water?—   150
Come, Kate, and wash, and welcome heartily.—
You whoreson villain, will you let it fall?
                       ⌜*He hits the Servant.*⌝

KATHERINE
Patience, I pray you, 'twas a fault unwilling.
PETRUCHIO
A whoreson beetle-headed flap-eared knave!—
Come, Kate, sit down. I know you have a stomach.   155
Will you give thanks, sweet Kate, or else shall I?—
What's this? Mutton?
FIRST SERVANT   Ay.
PETRUCHIO   Who brought it?
PETER   I.   160
PETRUCHIO   'Tis burnt, and so is all the meat.
What dogs are these? Where is the rascal cook?
How durst you, villains, bring it from the dresser
And serve it thus to me that love it not?
There, take it to you, trenchers, cups, and all!   165
      ⌜*He throws the food and dishes at them.*⌝
You heedless joltheads and unmannered slaves!
What, do you grumble? I'll be with you straight.
                      ⌜*The Servants exit.*⌝

KATHERINE
I pray you, husband, be not so disquiet.
The meat was well, if you were so contented.
PETRUCHIO
I tell thee, Kate, 'twas burnt and dried away,   170
And I expressly am forbid to touch it,
For it engenders choler, planteth anger,
And better 'twere that both of us did fast
(Since of ourselves, ourselves are choleric)
Than feed it with such over-roasted flesh.   175
Be patient. Tomorrow 't shall be mended,

180. **humor:** disposition

183. **continency:** self-restraint

184. **rails . . . rates:** i.e., scolds and berates; **that:** i.e., so that

188. **politicly:** shrewdly

190. **sharp:** hungry; **passing:** completely

191. **stoop:** fly directly to the keeper or to the prey

192. **lure:** the bait held by the keeper

193. **man my haggard:** train my falcon

195. **watch her:** force her to stay awake; **kites:** falcons

196. **bate:** beat their wings

203. **hurly:** commotion; **intend:** (1) pretend; (2) propose

A falconer and his tamed falcon. (4.1.190)
From George Turbeville, *The booke of faulconrie or hauking . . .* (1575).

And for this night we'll fast for company.
Come, I will bring thee to thy bridal chamber.
                                        They exit.

Enter Servants severally.

NATHANIEL   Peter, didst ever see the like?
PETER   He kills her in her own humor.   180

Enter Curtis.

GRUMIO   Where is he?
CURTIS   In her chamber,
    Making a sermon of continency to her,
    And rails and swears and rates, that she (poor soul)
    Knows not which way to stand, to look, to speak,   185
    And sits as one new-risen from a dream.
    Away, away, for he is coming hither!
                                ⌜*The Servants exit.*⌝

Enter Petruchio.

PETRUCHIO
    Thus have I politicly begun my reign,
    And 'tis my hope to end successfully.
    My falcon now is sharp and passing empty,   190
    And, till she stoop, she must not be full-gorged,
    For then she never looks upon her lure.
    Another way I have to man my haggard,
    To make her come and know her keeper's call.
    That is, to watch her, as we watch these kites   195
    That bate and beat and will not be obedient.
    She ate no meat today, nor none shall eat.
    Last night she slept not, nor tonight she shall not.
    As with the meat, some undeservèd fault
    I'll find about the making of the bed,   200
    And here I'll fling the pillow, there the bolster,
    This way the coverlet, another way the sheets.
    Ay, and amid this hurly I intend

204. **reverend:** respectful
205. **watch:** be kept awake
206. **rail and brawl:** scold and make noise
211. **shew:** reveal (a better way)

4.2 In Padua, Hortensio (as Litio) leads Tranio (as Lucentio) to spy on Bianca and Lucentio-Cambio as the couple kiss and talk of love. Hortensio, doffing his disguise as Litio, then rejects Bianca forever, resolves to marry a wealthy widow who loves him, and sets off to observe Petruchio's taming of Katherine. In the meantime, Biondello has found a traveling merchant whom Tranio persuades to impersonate Lucentio's father, Vincentio.

─────────

3. **bears . . . hand:** deceives me beautifully
4. **satisfy you in:** convince you of
7. **resolve:** answer
8. **that I profess:** that which I teach; **The Art to Love:** the *Ars Amatoria,* by the Roman poet Ovid
11. **proceeders:** workers (with wordplay on "proceeding" to an academic degree like master of arts, alluded to in line 9); **marry:** i.e., indeed

That all is done in reverend care of her.
And, in conclusion, she shall watch all night,   205
And, if she chance to nod, I'll rail and brawl,
And with the clamor keep her still awake.
This is a way to kill a wife with kindness.
And thus I'll curb her mad and headstrong humor.
He that knows better how to tame a shrew,   210
Now let him speak; 'tis charity to shew.

                                        He exits.

                    ⌜Scene 2⌝
Enter Tranio ⌜*as Lucentio*⌝ *and Hortensio* ⌜*as Litio.*⌝

TRANIO, ⌜*as* LUCENTIO⌝
  Is 't possible, friend Litio, that mistress Bianca
  Doth fancy any other but Lucentio?
  I tell you, sir, she bears me fair in hand.
⌜HORTENSIO, *as* LITIO⌝
  Sir, to satisfy you in what I have said,
  Stand by, and mark the manner of his teaching.   5
                              ⌜*They stand aside.*⌝

          Enter Bianca ⌜*and Lucentio as Cambio.*⌝

⌜LUCENTIO, *as* CAMBIO⌝
  Now mistress, profit you in what you read?
BIANCA
  What, master, read you? First resolve me that.
⌜LUCENTIO, *as* CAMBIO⌝
  I read that I profess, *The Art to Love.*
BIANCA
  And may you prove, sir, master of your art.
LUCENTIO, ⌜*as* CAMBIO⌝
  While you, sweet dear, prove mistress of my heart.   10
                  ⌜*They move aside and kiss and talk.*⌝
HORTENSIO, ⌜*as* LITIO⌝
  Quick proceeders, marry! Now tell me, I pray,

                        153

15. **wonderful:** astounding
18. **scorn:** i.e., scorns
20. **cullion:** low fellow (term of contempt)
24. **lightness:** inconstancy
31. **fondly:** foolishly; **withal:** i.e., with
34. **beastly:** shamelessly
35. **but he:** i.e., except "Cambio"
38. **Ere:** before; **which:** i.e., who (i.e., the widow)
39. **haggard:** a wild female hawk

You that durst swear that your mistress Bianca
Loved ⌜none⌝ in the world so well as Lucentio.
TRANIO, ⌜as LUCENTIO⌝
  O despiteful love, unconstant womankind!
  I tell thee, Litio, this is wonderful!   15
HORTENSIO
  Mistake no more. I am not Litio,
  Nor a musician as I seem to be,
  But one that scorn to live in this disguise
  For such a one as leaves a gentleman
  And makes a god of such a cullion.   20
  Know, sir, that I am called Hortensio.
TRANIO, ⌜as LUCENTIO⌝
  Signior Hortensio, I have often heard
  Of your entire affection to Bianca,
  And since mine eyes are witness of her lightness,
  I will with you, if you be so contented,   25
  Forswear Bianca and her love forever.
HORTENSIO
  See how they kiss and court! Signior Lucentio,
  Here is my hand, and here I firmly vow
  Never to woo her more, but do forswear her
  As one unworthy all the former favors   30
  That I have fondly flattered ⌜her⌝ withal.
TRANIO, ⌜as LUCENTIO⌝
  And here I take the like unfeignèd oath,
  Never to marry with her, though she would entreat.
  Fie on her, see how beastly she doth court him!
HORTENSIO
  Would all the world but he had quite forsworn!   35
  For me, that I may surely keep mine oath,
  I will be married to a wealthy widow
  Ere three days pass, which hath as long loved me
  As I have loved this proud disdainful haggard.
  And so farewell, Signior Lucentio.   40
  Kindness in women, not their beauteous looks,

155

45. **'longeth:** i.e., belongeth

59. **eleven and twenty long:** i.e., exactly right (The allusion is to the card game "Thirty-one.")

60. **charm:** magically silence

63. **ancient angel:** i.e., reliable old man (literally, a coin [**angel**] whose value is above suspicion, unlike that of newer coins)

64. **serve the turn:** suit the purpose

Shall win my love, and so I take my leave,
In resolution as I swore before.
⌈*Hortensio exits;*
Bianca and Lucentio come forward.⌉

TRANIO
Mistress Bianca, bless you with such grace
As 'longeth to a lover's blessèd case!   45
Nay, I have ta'en you napping, gentle love,
And have forsworn you with Hortensio.

BIANCA
Tranio, you jest. But have you both forsworn me?

TRANIO
Mistress, we have.

LUCENTIO   Then we are rid of Litio.   50

TRANIO
I' faith, he'll have a lusty widow now
That shall be wooed and wedded in a day.

BIANCA   God give him joy.

TRANIO
Ay, and he'll tame her.

BIANCA   He says so, Tranio?   55

TRANIO
Faith, he is gone unto the taming school.

BIANCA
The taming school? What, is there such a place?

TRANIO
Ay, mistress, and Petruchio is the master,
That teacheth tricks eleven and twenty long
To tame a shrew and charm her chattering tongue.   60

Enter Biondello

BIONDELLO
O master, master, I have watched so long
That I am dog-weary, but at last I spied
An ancient angel coming down the hill
Will serve the turn.

66. **marcantant:** Biondello's version of *merca-tante*, Italian for "merchant"

72. **give assurance:** i.e., provide guarantees of the dowry that Tranio (as Lucentio) has promised

74 SD. Although the Folio has this character enter and speak under the designation "Pedant," his words (lines 94–95) suggest that he is no pedant (school-master), but is rather Biondello's **marcantant,** or merchant. We have therefore followed editor Ann Thompson in emending "Pedant" to "Merchant" throughout.

77. **far on:** i.e., farther on; **the farthest:** i.e., the end of your journey

81. **What countryman:** i.e., from what country are you?

84. **careless:** without regard for

85. **goes hard:** is serious

88. **stayed:** detained

TRANIO   What is he, Biondello?   65
BIONDELLO
   Master, a marcantant, or a pedant,
   I know not what, but formal in apparel,
   In gait and countenance surely like a father.
LUCENTIO   And what of him, Tranio?
TRANIO
   If he be credulous, and trust my tale,   70
   I'll make him glad to seem Vincentio
   And give assurance to Baptista Minola
   As if he were the right Vincentio.
   Take ⌜in⌝ your love, and then let me alone.
                              ⌜Lucentio and Bianca exit.⌝

                    Enter a ⌜Merchant.⌝

⌜MERCHANT⌝
   God save you, sir.   75
TRANIO, ⌜as LUCENTIO⌝ And you, sir. You are welcome.
   Travel you far on, or are you at the farthest?
⌜MERCHANT⌝
   Sir, at the farthest for a week or two,
   But then up farther, and as far as Rome,
   And so to Tripoli, if God lend me life.   80
TRANIO, ⌜as LUCENTIO⌝
   What countryman, I pray?
⌜MERCHANT⌝   Of Mantua.
TRANIO, ⌜as LUCENTIO⌝
   Of Mantua, sir? Marry, God forbid!
   And come to Padua, careless of your life?
⌜MERCHANT⌝
   My life, sir? How, I pray? For that goes hard.   85
TRANIO, ⌜as LUCENTIO⌝
   'Tis death for anyone in Mantua
   To come to Padua. Know you not the cause?
   Your ships are stayed at Venice, and the Duke,
   For private quarrel 'twixt your duke and him,

90. **it:** i.e., the death sentence upon citizens of Mantua

91. **but . . . but:** except . . . only

92. **else:** otherwise

94. **bills . . . exchange:** papers to be exchanged for money

100. **grave:** worthy and serious

104. **sooth:** truth

107. **all one:** no matter

111. **are like to:** i.e., look like

112. **credit:** reputation; **undertake:** take on, assume

114. **take . . . should:** i.e., be careful to assume the proper manner

117. **accept of:** i.e., accept

Hath published and proclaimed it openly.   90
'Tis marvel, but that you are but newly come,
You might have heard it else proclaimed about.
⌜MERCHANT⌝
    Alas, sir, it is worse for me than so,
    For I have bills for money by exchange
    From Florence, and must here deliver them.   95
TRANIO, ⌜as LUCENTIO⌝
    Well, sir, to do you courtesy,
    This will I do, and this I will advise you.
    First tell me, have you ever been at Pisa?
⌜MERCHANT⌝
    Ay, sir, in Pisa have I often been,
    Pisa renownèd for grave citizens.   100
TRANIO, ⌜as LUCENTIO⌝
    Among them know you one Vincentio?
⌜MERCHANT⌝
    I know him not, but I have heard of him:
    A merchant of incomparable wealth.
TRANIO, ⌜as LUCENTIO⌝
    He is my father, sir, and sooth to say,
    In count'nance somewhat doth resemble you.   105
BIONDELLO, ⌜aside⌝ As much as an apple doth an
    oyster, and all one.
TRANIO, ⌜as LUCENTIO⌝
    To save your life in this extremity,
    This favor will I do you for his sake
    (And think it not the worst of all your fortunes   110
    That you are like to Sir Vincentio):
    His name and credit shall you undertake,
    And in my house you shall be friendly lodged.
    Look that you take upon you as you should.
    You understand me, sir. So shall you stay   115
    Till you have done your business in the city.
    If this be court'sy, sir, accept of it.

118. **repute:** consider
120. **make . . . good:** carry out the plan
123. **pass assurance of:** formally guarantee

4.3 At Petruchio's home, Grumio torments Katherine by promising her food that he fails to bring. Petruchio then serves Katherine himself, demanding her thanks. The Haberdasher and Tailor bring in the cap and gown that Katherine plans to wear for Bianca's wedding feast, but Petruchio refuses them. Petruchio threatens that she may not return to her father's for Bianca's wedding feast unless Katherine agrees with everything he says, no matter how self-evidently false it is.

---

2. **my wrong:** the wrong that I suffer
5. **present:** immediate
8. **needed . . . should:** i.e., needed to
9. **meat:** food
11. **spites:** angers; **wants:** deprivations
13. **As who should say:** i.e., as if to say
16. **so it be:** i.e., so long as it is
17. **neat's:** calf's

⌜MERCHANT⌝
    O sir, I do, and will repute you ever
    The patron of my life and liberty.
TRANIO, ⌜as LUCENTIO⌝
    Then go with me, to make the matter good.   120
    This, by the way, I let you understand:
    My father is here looked for every day
    To pass assurance of a dower in marriage
    'Twixt me and one Baptista's daughter here.
    In all these circumstances I'll instruct you.   125
    Go with me to clothe you as becomes you.
                                                    They exit.

⌜Scene 3⌝
Enter Katherine and Grumio.

GRUMIO
    No, no, forsooth, I dare not for my life.
KATHERINE
    The more my wrong, the more his spite appears.
    What, did he marry me to famish me?
    Beggars that come unto my father's door
    Upon entreaty have a present alms.   5
    If not, elsewhere they meet with charity.
    But I, who never knew how to entreat,
    Nor never needed that I should entreat,
    Am starved for meat, giddy for lack of sleep,
    With oaths kept waking and with brawling fed.   10
    And that which spites me more than all these wants,
    He does it under name of perfect love,
    As who should say, if I should sleep or eat
    'Twere deadly sickness or else present death.
    I prithee, go, and get me some repast,   15
    I care not what, so it be wholesome food.
GRUMIO   What say you to a neat's foot?

18. **passing:** very
19. **choleric:** liable to promote choler (see 4.1.172)
26. **let . . . rest:** i.e., do without the mustard
32. **the very name:** only the name
33. **Sorrow on thee:** i.e., may sorrow come upon thee
36. **all amort:** (French: *à la mort*) dejected

KATHERINE
  'Tis passing good. I prithee let me have it.
GRUMIO
  I fear it is too choleric a meat.
  How say you to a fat tripe finely broiled?   20
KATHERINE
  I like it well. Good Grumio, fetch it me.
GRUMIO
  I cannot tell. I fear 'tis choleric.
  What say you to a piece of beef and mustard?
KATHERINE
  A dish that I do love to feed upon.
GRUMIO
  Ay, but the mustard is too hot a little.   25
KATHERINE
  Why then, the beef, and let the mustard rest.
GRUMIO
  Nay then, I will not. You shall have the mustard
  Or else you get no beef of Grumio.
KATHERINE
  Then both, or one, or any thing thou wilt.
GRUMIO
  Why then, the mustard without the beef.   30
KATHERINE
  Go, get thee gone, thou false deluding slave,
                              ⌜She⌝ beats him.
  That feed'st me with the very name of meat.
  Sorrow on thee, and all the pack of you
  That triumph thus upon my misery.
  Go, get thee gone, I say.   35

          Enter Petruchio and Hortensio with meat.

PETRUCHIO
  How fares my Kate? What, sweeting, all amort?
HORTENSIO
  Mistress, what cheer?
KATHERINE   Faith, as cold as can be.

41. **dress thy meat:** prepare your food
44. **is sorted to no proof:** i.e., turn out to have no effect
46. **stand:** i.e., stay
54. **apace:** right now, immediately
57. **bravely:** splendidly (in our dress)
59. **ruffs:** starched wheel-like collars; **farthingales:** hooped petticoats
60. **brav'ry:** splendid dress
61. **knav'ry:** i.e., nonsense
62. **stays thy leisure:** i.e., awaits your pleasure
63. **ruffling:** i.e., ruffled

A woman wearing a farthingale. (4.3.59)
From John Speed, *The theatre of the empire . . .* (1614).

166

PETRUCHIO
   Pluck up thy spirits. Look cheerfully upon me.
   Here, love, thou seest how diligent I am,   40
   To dress thy meat myself and bring it thee.
   I am sure, sweet Kate, this kindness merits thanks.
   What, not a word? Nay then, thou lov'st it not,
   And all my pains is sorted to no proof.
   Here, take away this dish.   45
KATHERINE   I pray you, let it stand.
PETRUCHIO
   The poorest service is repaid with thanks,
   And so shall mine before you touch the meat.
KATHERINE   I thank you, sir.
HORTENSIO
   Signior Petruchio, fie, you are to blame.   50
   Come, Mistress Kate, I'll bear you company.
PETRUCHIO, ⌈aside to Hortensio⌉
   Eat it up all, Hortensio, if thou lovest me.—
   Much good do it unto thy gentle heart.
   Kate, eat apace.
                  ⌈Katherine and Hortensio prepare to eat.⌉
                           And now, my honey love,   55
   Will we return unto thy father's house
   And revel it as bravely as the best,
   With silken coats and caps and golden rings,
   With ruffs and cuffs and farthingales and things,
   With scarves and fans and double change of brav'ry,   60
   With amber bracelets, beads, and all this knav'ry.
   What, hast thou dined? The tailor stays thy leisure
   To deck thy body with his ruffling treasure.

                        Enter Tailor.

   Come, tailor, let us see these ornaments.
   Lay forth the gown.   65

                     Enter Haberdasher.

                     What news with you, sir?

167

67. **bespeak:** order
68. **porringer:** porridge bowl
69. **lewd:** low, vulgar; **filthy:** mean, disgusting
70. **cockle:** cockleshell
71. **knack:** knickknack; **toy, trick:** both mean "trifle," something worthless
73. **fit the time:** is fashionable now
78. **leave:** permission
87. **custard-coffin:** crust for a custard
92. **masking-stuff:** costumes for maskers (i.e., people who came to parties wearing disguises)

⌜HABERDASHER⌝
Here is the cap your Worship did bespeak.
PETRUCHIO
Why, this was molded on a porringer!
A velvet dish! Fie, fie, 'tis lewd and filthy.
Why, 'tis a cockle or a walnut shell,   70
A knack, a toy, a trick, a baby's cap.
Away with it! Come, let me have a bigger.
KATHERINE
I'll have no bigger. This doth fit the time,
And gentlewomen wear such caps as these.
PETRUCHIO
When you are gentle, you shall have one too,   75
And not till then.
HORTENSIO, ⌜aside⌝ That will not be in haste.
KATHERINE
Why, sir, I trust I may have leave to speak,
And speak I will. I am no child, no babe.
Your betters have endured me say my mind,   80
And if you cannot, best you stop your ears.
My tongue will tell the anger of my heart,
Or else my heart, concealing it, will break,
And, rather than it shall, I will be free
Even to the uttermost, as I please, in words.   85
PETRUCHIO
Why, thou sayst true. It is ⌜a⌝ paltry cap,
A custard-coffin, a bauble, a silken pie.
I love thee well in that thou lik'st it not.
KATHERINE
Love me, or love me not, I like the cap,
And it I will have, or I will have none.   90
                              ⌜Exit Haberdasher.⌝
PETRUCHIO
Thy gown? Why, ay. Come, tailor, let us see 't.
O mercy God, what masking-stuff is here?

93. **demi-cannon:** large cannon

94. **carved . . . tart:** i.e., with slits like the upper crust of a pie

96. **censer:** perhaps, incense burner

98. **like:** i.e., likely

101. **Marry, and did:** i.e., indeed I did; **be remembered:** i.e., remember

103. **hop . . . kennel:** i.e., hop over every gutter

104. **custom:** trade, patronage

107. **quaint:** elegant

108. **commendable:** accent on first syllable

109. **Belike:** perhaps; **puppet:** plaything

115. **yard:** yardstick; **quarter:** quarter-yard; **nail:** one-sixteenth yard

116. **nit:** louse egg

117. **Braved:** defied; **with:** i.e., by

119. **be-mete:** intensive form of **mete,** meaning "measure"; i.e., measure thoroughly; beat you

120. **As . . . liv'st:** i.e., remembering this thrashing, you will think before chattering as long as you live

What's this? A sleeve? 'Tis like ⌜a⌝ demi-cannon.
What, up and down carved like an apple tart?
Here's snip and nip and cut and slish and slash,   95
Like to a censer in a barber's shop.
Why, what a devil's name, tailor, call'st thou this?
HORTENSIO, ⌜aside⌝
I see she's like to have neither cap nor gown.
TAILOR
You bid me make it orderly and well,
According to the fashion and the time.   100
PETRUCHIO
Marry, and did. But if you be remembered,
I did not bid you mar it to the time.
Go, hop me over every kennel home,
For you shall hop without my custom, sir.
I'll none of it. Hence, make your best of it.   105
KATHERINE
I never saw a better-fashioned gown,
More quaint, more pleasing, nor more
    commendable.
Belike you mean to make a puppet of me.
PETRUCHIO
Why, true, he means to make a puppet of thee.   110
TAILOR
She says your Worship means to make a puppet of
    her.
PETRUCHIO
O monstrous arrogance! Thou liest, thou thread,
    thou thimble,
Thou yard, three-quarters, half-yard, quarter, nail!   115
Thou flea, thou nit, thou winter cricket, thou!
Braved in mine own house with a skein of thread?
Away, thou rag, thou quantity, thou remnant,
Or I shall so be-mete thee with thy yard
As thou shalt think on prating whilst thou liv'st.   120
I tell thee, I, that thou hast marred her gown.

123. **had direction:** i.e., was directed

125. **stuff:** material (for the gown)

129. **faced:** (1) sewed on trim; (2) defied

131. **braved:** made to look splendid

132. **brave:** defy

134. **Ergo:** Latin for "therefore"

136. **note . . . fashion:** written instruction for the style of the gown

138. **in 's:** in his

139. **Imprimis:** Latin for "first"

142. **bottom:** ball or skein

144. **small-compassed:** i.e., in the form of a small semicircle

146. **trunk sleeve:** wide sleeve

148. **curiously:** exquisitely

152. **prove upon thee:** i.e., make good in a fight

"A loose-bodied gown." (4.3.139)
From Cesare Vecellio, *Degli habiti antichi . . .* (1590).

TAILOR
Your Worship is deceived. The gown is made
Just as my master had direction.
Grumio gave order how it should be done.

GRUMIO I gave him no order. I gave him the stuff.   125

TAILOR
But how did you desire it should be made?

GRUMIO Marry, sir, with needle and thread.

TAILOR
But did you not request to have it cut?

GRUMIO Thou hast faced many things.

TAILOR I have.   130

GRUMIO Face not me. Thou hast braved many men;
brave not me. I will neither be faced nor braved. I
say unto thee, I bid thy master cut out the gown,
but I did not bid him cut it to pieces. *Ergo*, thou
liest.   135

TAILOR Why, here is the note of the fashion to testify.
⌐*He shows a paper.*⌐

PETRUCHIO Read it.

GRUMIO The note lies in 's throat, if he say I said so.

TAILOR ⌐*reads*⌐ "*Imprimis*, a loose-bodied gown—"

GRUMIO Master, if ever I said "loose-bodied gown,"   140
sew me in the skirts of it and beat me to death with
a bottom of brown thread. I said "a gown."

PETRUCHIO Proceed.

TAILOR ⌐*reads*⌐ "With a small-compassed cape—"

GRUMIO I confess the cape.   145

TAILOR ⌐*reads*⌐ "With a trunk sleeve—"

GRUMIO I confess two sleeves.

TAILOR ⌐*reads*⌐ "The sleeves curiously cut."

PETRUCHIO Ay, there's the villainy.

GRUMIO Error i' th' bill, sir, error i' th' bill! I com-   150
manded the sleeves should be cut out and sewed
up again, and that I'll prove upon thee, though thy
little finger be armed in a thimble.

154. **An:** i.e., if

154–55. **place where:** a suitable place

156. **straight:** straightway, immediately; **bill:** (1) note; (2) long-handled weapon

157. **mete-yard:** measuring stick

159. **odds:** i.e., advantage

162. **unto . . . use:** i.e., for your master to use

165. **what's . . . that:** i.e., what do you mean by that

173. **of:** i.e., at

176. **mean habiliments:** common clothes

180. **peereth in:** i.e., shows through; **habit:** clothes

181. **What:** interjection at the beginning of a question or exclamation

TAILOR   This is true that I say. An I had thee in place
  where, thou shouldst know it.   155
GRUMIO   I am for thee straight. Take thou the bill, give
  me thy mete-yard, and spare not me.
HORTENSIO   God-a-mercy, Grumio, then he shall have
  no odds.
PETRUCHIO
  Well, sir, in brief, the gown is not for me.   160
GRUMIO   You are i' th' right, sir, 'tis for my mistress.
PETRUCHIO
  Go, take it up unto thy master's use.
GRUMIO   Villain, not for thy life! Take up my mistress'
  gown for thy master's use!
PETRUCHIO   Why, sir, what's your conceit in that?   165
GRUMIO   O, sir, the conceit is deeper than you think
  for. Take up my mistress' gown to his master's use!
  O, fie, fie, fie!
PETRUCHIO, ⌈*aside to Hortensio*⌉
  Hortensio, say thou wilt see the tailor paid.
  ⌈*To Tailor.*⌉ Go, take it hence. Begone, and say no   170
  more.
HORTENSIO, ⌈*aside to Tailor*⌉
  Tailor, I'll pay thee for thy gown tomorrow.
  Take no unkindness of his hasty words.
  Away, I say. Commend me to thy master.
                                      Tailor exits.
PETRUCHIO
  Well, come, my Kate, we will unto your father's,   175
  Even in these honest mean habiliments.
  Our purses shall be proud, our garments poor,
  For 'tis the mind that makes the body rich,
  And as the sun breaks through the darkest clouds,
  So honor peereth in the meanest habit.   180
  What, is the jay more precious than the lark
  Because his feathers are more beautiful?
  Or is the adder better than the eel

186. **furniture:** accessories; **mean array:** ordinary clothes

189. **sport:** i.e., disport, entertain ourselves

194. **some:** i.e., about

195. **dinner time:** i.e., noon

199. **Look what:** i.e., whatever

200. **still:** always; **crossing:** opposing; **let 't alone:** i.e., abandon preparations for departure

---

4.4 In Padua, the Merchant impersonating Vincentio visits Baptista with Tranio, who is still disguised as Lucentio. Baptista accepts the Merchant's guarantee of Bianca's dowry and sends "Cambio" to Bianca to tell her the marriage plans. Meanwhile, Baptista arranges to visit "Lucentio" and "Vincentio" at their lodging to finalize the marriage contract. Biondello tells Lucentio that all the arrangements have been made for Lucentio to elope with Bianca.

---

0 SD. **booted:** in riding boots

2. **And but:** unless (The Merchant may be practicing his role as Vincentio.)

4. **Near:** i.e., nearly

5. **Pegasus:** i.e., an inn named after the mythical winged horse

Because his painted skin contents the eye?
O no, good Kate. Neither art thou the worse   185
For this poor furniture and mean array.
If thou ⌜account'st⌝ it shame, lay it on me,
And therefore frolic! We will hence forthwith
To feast and sport us at thy father's house.
⌜To Grumio.⌝ Go, call my men, and let us straight to   190
     him,
And bring our horses unto Long-lane end.
There will we mount, and thither walk on foot.
Let's see, I think 'tis now some seven o'clock,
And well we may come there by dinner time.   195

KATHERINE
I dare assure you, sir, 'tis almost two,
And 'twill be supper time ere you come there.

PETRUCHIO
It shall be seven ere I go to horse.
Look what I speak, or do, or think to do,
You are still crossing it. Sirs, let 't alone.   200
I will not go today, and, ere I do,
It shall be what o'clock I say it is.

HORTENSIO, ⌜aside⌝
Why, so, this gallant will command the sun!
                              ⌜They exit.⌝

                    ⌜Scene 4⌝
Enter Tranio ⌜as Lucentio,⌝ and the ⌜Merchant,⌝ booted,
           and dressed like Vincentio.

TRANIO, ⌜as LUCENTIO⌝
⌜Sir,⌝ this is the house. Please it you that I call?

⌜MERCHANT⌝
Ay, what else? And but I be deceived,
Signior Baptista may remember me,
Near twenty years ago, in Genoa,
Where we were lodgers at the Pegasus.   5

                      177

7. **'longeth:** i.e., belongeth
10. **schooled:** instructed
12. **throughly:** thoroughly
13. **right:** true
18. **tall:** fine, bold
20. **happily:** opportunely
24. **Soft:** i.e., enough, hush
25. **by your leave:** a polite phrase
27. **weighty cause:** serious matter

TRANIO, ⌜*as* LUCENTIO⌝
　'Tis well. And hold your own in any case
　With such austerity as 'longeth to a father.
⌜MERCHANT⌝
　I warrant you.

Enter Biondello.

　　　　　　　But, sir, here comes your boy.
　'Twere good he were schooled.   10
TRANIO, ⌜*as* LUCENTIO⌝
　Fear you not him.—Sirrah Biondello,
　Now do your duty throughly, I advise you.
　Imagine 'twere the right Vincentio.
BIONDELLO　Tut, fear not me.
TRANIO, ⌜*as* LUCENTIO⌝
　But hast thou done thy errand to Baptista?   15
BIONDELLO
　I told him that your father was at Venice,
　And that you looked for him this day in Padua.
TRANIO, ⌜*as* LUCENTIO⌝
　Thou'rt a tall fellow. Hold thee that to drink.
　　　　　　　　　⌜*He gives him money.*⌝

Enter Baptista and Lucentio ⌜*as Cambio.*⌝

　Here comes Baptista. Set your countenance, sir.
　　　　　　　⌜*Merchant stands*⌝ *bareheaded.*
TRANIO, ⌜*as* LUCENTIO⌝
　Signior Baptista, you are happily met.—   20
　Sir, this is the gentleman I told you of.
　I pray you stand good father to me now.
　Give me Bianca for my patrimony.
⌜MERCHANT, *as* VINCENTIO⌝　Soft, son.—
　Sir, by your leave, having come to Padua   25
　To gather in some debts, my son Lucentio
　Made me acquainted with a weighty cause
　Of love between your daughter and himself.

29, 30. **for:** because of

31. **stay:** delay

32. **in . . . care:** i.e., with the care that a good father ought to have

37. **curious:** overparticular, too demanding

46. **pass:** transfer to

50. **affied:** formally betrothed; **such assurance ta'en:** such guarantees provided

51. **either part's agreement:** what each party has agreed to

53. **Pitchers have ears:** i.e., we might be overheard (proverbial)

54. **heark'ning still:** listening constantly

55. **happily:** perhaps

56. **an it like you:** i.e., if it please you

57. **lie:** stay

58. **pass:** i.e., transact

And, for the good report I hear of you,
And for the love he beareth to your daughter   30
And she to him, to stay him not too long,
I am content, in a good father's care,
To have him matched. And if you please to like
No worse than I, upon some agreement
Me shall you find ready and willing   35
With one consent to have her so bestowed,
For curious I cannot be with you,
Signior Baptista, of whom I hear so well.
BAPTISTA
Sir, pardon me in what I have to say.
Your plainness and your shortness please me well.   40
Right true it is your son Lucentio here
Doth love my daughter, and she loveth him,
Or both dissemble deeply their affections.
And therefore, if you say no more than this,
That like a father you will deal with him   45
And pass my daughter a sufficient dower,
The match is made, and all is done.
Your son shall have my daughter with consent.
TRANIO, ⌜as LUCENTIO⌝
I thank you, sir. Where then do you know best
We be affied and such assurance ta'en   50
As shall with either part's agreement stand?
BAPTISTA
Not in my house, Lucentio, for you know
Pitchers have ears, and I have many servants.
Besides, old Gremio is heark'ning still,
And happily we might be interrupted.   55
TRANIO, ⌜as LUCENTIO⌝
Then at my lodging, an it like you.
There doth my father lie, and there this night
We'll pass the business privately and well.
Send for your daughter by your servant here.
          ⌜He indicates Lucentio, and winks at him.⌝

60. **scrivener:** notary public
61. **slender warning:** short notice
62. **pittance:** i.e., refreshment
63. **likes:** pleases; **hie you:** hurry
64. **straight:** straightway, immediately
67. **like:** i.e., likely
71. **mess:** dish; **cheer:** food and drink
79. **'has:** i.e., he has
82. **moralize:** i.e., explain

My boy shall fetch the scrivener presently.   60
The worst is this: that at so slender warning
You are like to have a thin and slender pittance.
BAPTISTA
It likes me well.—Cambio, hie you home,
And bid Bianca make her ready straight.
And, if you will, tell what hath happenèd: 65
Lucentio's father is arrived in Padua,
And how she's like to be Lucentio's wife.
⌜*Lucentio exits.*⌝

BIONDELLO
I pray the gods she may, with all my heart.
TRANIO, ⌜*as* LUCENTIO⌝
Dally not with the gods, but get thee gone.—
Signior Baptista, shall I lead the way?   70
Welcome! One mess is like to be your cheer.
Come, sir, we will better it in Pisa.
BAPTISTA   I follow you.
                    ⌜*All but Biondello*⌝ *exit.*

                    Enter Lucentio.

BIONDELLO   Cambio.
LUCENTIO   What sayst thou, Biondello?   75
BIONDELLO   You saw my master wink and laugh upon
    you?
LUCENTIO   Biondello, what of that?
BIONDELLO   Faith, nothing; but 'has left me here be-
    hind to expound the meaning or moral of his signs   80
    and tokens.
LUCENTIO   I pray thee, moralize them.
BIONDELLO   Then thus: Baptista is safe, talking with
    the deceiving father of a deceitful son.
LUCENTIO   And what of him?   85
BIONDELLO   His daughter is to be brought by you to the
    supper.

93. **assurance:** marriage contract

93–94. **Take . . . of her:** i.e., make sure of her

94. **cum . . . solum:** "with the exclusive right to print," a formula often appearing on the title pages of books in this period (Biondello plays with the formula as a description of legal marriage.)

97. **that:** i.e., what

101. **tarry:** wait

105–6. **against you come:** in preparation for your coming

106. **appendix:** appendage (spouse)

108. **wherefore:** why

110. **Hap what hap may:** i.e., whatever may happen; **roundly . . . her:** perhaps, approach her boldly

111. **shall go hard:** i.e., will not be for lack of effort

4.5 Katherine now gives assent to every word Petruchio says. On their way to her father's, they meet the true Vincentio, who is going to Padua to visit his son. They travel together to Padua.

1–2. **our father's:** i.e., Baptista's

LUCENTIO   And then?
BIONDELLO   The old priest at Saint Luke's Church is at
   your command at all hours.   90
LUCENTIO   And what of all this?
BIONDELLO   I cannot tell, ⌈except⌉ they are busied
   about a counterfeit assurance. Take you assurance
   of her *cum privilegio ad imprimendum solum*. To th'
   church take the priest, clerk, and some sufficient   95
   honest witnesses.
      If this be not that you look for, I have no more to
      say,
   But bid Bianca farewell forever and a day.
LUCENTIO   Hear'st thou, Biondello?   100
BIONDELLO   I cannot tarry. I knew a wench married in
   an afternoon as she went to the garden for parsley
   to stuff a rabbit, and so may you, sir. And so adieu,
   sir. My master hath appointed me to go to Saint
   Luke's to bid the priest be ready to come against   105
   you come with your appendix.   *He exits.*
LUCENTIO
   I may, and will, if she be so contented.
   She will be pleased. Then wherefore should I
      doubt?
   Hap what hap may, I'll roundly go about her.   110
   It shall go hard if "Cambio" go without her.
                                             He exits.

                        ⌈Scene 5⌉
   Enter Petruchio, Katherine, Hortensio, ⌈and Servants.⌉

PETRUCHIO
   Come on, i' God's name, once more toward our
      father's.
   Good Lord, how bright and goodly shines the moon!
KATHERINE
   The moon? The sun! It is not moonlight now.

                          185

8. **list:** choose; or, please

9. **Or e'er I:** before I ever will

12. **crossed:** opposed, contradicted

16. **rush candle:** cheap candle made by dipping a rush in grease or fat

26. **field:** i.e., battlefield

27–28. **Thus . . . bias:** Petruchio claims that Katherine is now acting naturally, no longer being perverse. (In the game of bowls, the ball is weighted so that it follows a curved path [its **bias**]; **against the bias,** thus, means "off its natural course.")

29. **soft:** i.e., wait a minute

PETRUCHIO
　I say it is the moon that shines so bright.　　　　5
KATHERINE
　I know it is the sun that shines so bright.
PETRUCHIO
　Now, by my mother's son, and that's myself,
　It shall be moon, or star, or what I list,
　Or e'er I journey to your father's house.
　⌜*To Servants.*⌝ Go on, and fetch our horses back　　10
　　again.—
　Evermore crossed and crossed, nothing but crossed!
HORTENSIO, ⌜*to Katherine*⌝
　Say as he says, or we shall never go.
KATHERINE
　Forward, I pray, since we have come so far,
　And be it moon, or sun, or what you please.　　15
　And if you please to call it a rush candle,
　Henceforth I vow it shall be so for me.
PETRUCHIO　I say it is the moon.
KATHERINE　I know it is the moon.
PETRUCHIO
　Nay, then you lie. It is the blessèd sun.　　20
KATHERINE
　Then God be blest, it ⌜is⌝ the blessèd sun.
　But sun it is not, when you say it is not,
　And the moon changes even as your mind.
　What you will have it named, even that it is,
　And so it shall be so for Katherine.　　25
HORTENSIO
　Petruchio, go thy ways, the field is won.
PETRUCHIO
　Well, forward, forward. Thus the bowl should run,
　And not unluckily against the bias.
　But soft! Company is coming here.

　　　　　　　Enter Vincentio.

187

30–31. **where away:** i.e., where are you going?

33. **fresher:** more radiant

34. **war . . . red:** language typical of love poetry of the period as it described womanly beauty

36. **become:** fit

42. **Whither away:** i.e., where are you going?

44–45. **whom . . . thee:** i.e., to whom you have been given by fortune   **Allots:** i.e., allot

51. **green:** i.e., young, fresh

52. **reverend:** worthy of respect

54. **withal:** in addition

58. **encounter:** i.e., greeting; **amazed:** astounded

⌐*To Vincentio.*⌐ Good morrow, gentle mistress, where   30
  away?—
Tell me, sweet Kate, and tell me truly, too,
Hast thou beheld a fresher gentlewoman?
Such war of white and red within her cheeks!
What stars do spangle heaven with such beauty   35
As those two eyes become that heavenly face?—
Fair lovely maid, once more good day to thee.—
Sweet Kate, embrace her for her beauty's sake.
HORTENSIO, ⌐*aside*⌐
He will make the man mad, to make the woman of
  him.   40
KATHERINE
Young budding virgin, fair and fresh and sweet,
Whither away, or ⌐where⌐ is thy abode?
Happy the parents of so fair a child!
Happier the man whom favorable stars
⌐Allots⌐ thee for his lovely bedfellow.   45
PETRUCHIO
Why, how now, Kate? I hope thou art not mad!
This is a man—old, wrinkled, faded, withered—
And not a maiden, as thou sayst he is.
KATHERINE
Pardon, old father, my mistaking eyes
That have been so bedazzled with the sun   50
That everything I look on seemeth green.
Now I perceive thou art a reverend father.
Pardon, I pray thee, for my mad mistaking.
PETRUCHIO
Do, good old grandsire, and withal make known
Which way thou travelest. If along with us,   55
We shall be joyful of thy company.
VINCENTIO
Fair sir, and you, my merry mistress,
That with your strange encounter much amazed me,
My name is called Vincentio, my dwelling Pisa,

68. **by this:** by now
69. **esteem:** repute
71. **so qualified:** with such qualities; **beseem:** suit, become
75. **of:** i.e., at, with
76. **else:** instead
77. **pleasant:** merry; **break a jest:** play a joke
80. **hereof:** of it
81. **merriment:** joke; **jealous:** suspicious
82. **in heart:** in good spirits
83. **Have to:** i.e., now for; **froward:** perverse
84. **untoward:** stubborn, intractable

And bound I am to Padua, there to visit   60
A son of mine which long I have not seen.
PETRUCHIO
What is his name?
VINCENTIO   Lucentio, gentle sir.
PETRUCHIO
Happily met, the happier for thy son.
And now by law as well as reverend age,   65
I may entitle thee my loving father.
The sister to my wife, this gentlewoman,
Thy son by this hath married. Wonder not,
Nor be not grieved. She is of good esteem,
Her dowry wealthy, and of worthy birth;   70
Beside, so qualified as may beseem
The spouse of any noble gentleman.
Let me embrace with old Vincentio,
And wander we to see thy honest son,
Who will of thy arrival be full joyous.   75
VINCENTIO
But is this true, or is it else your pleasure,
Like pleasant travelers, to break a jest
Upon the company you overtake?
HORTENSIO
I do assure thee, father, so it is.
PETRUCHIO
Come, go along and see the truth hereof,   80
For our first merriment hath made thee jealous.
                    ⌜*All but Hortensio*⌝ *exit.*
HORTENSIO
Well, Petruchio, this has put me in heart!
Have to my widow, and if she ⌜be⌝ froward,
Then hast thou taught Hortensio to be untoward.
                              He exits.

THE
TAMING
OF THE
SHREW

ACT 5

5.1 After Bianca has secretly married Lucentio, Petruchio, Katherine, and Lucentio's father arrive at Lucentio's lodging. They are rebuffed by the Merchant impersonating Vincentio. Vincentio denounces as frauds the Merchant and then Tranio, who turns up still disguised as Lucentio. As Vincentio is about to be carried off to jail by an officer, the true Lucentio arrives with his bride, successfully begs his father's pardon for the secret marriage, and explains the disguises.

---

10. **bears more toward:** is closer to
14. **cheer is toward:** refreshment can be expected

⌜ACT 5⌝

⌜Scene 1⌝

Enter Biondello, Lucentio ⌜as himself,⌝ and Bianca.
Gremio is out before ⌜and stands to the side.⌝

BIONDELLO Softly and swiftly, sir, for the priest is
ready.
LUCENTIO I fly, Biondello. But they may chance to
need thee at home. Therefore leave us.
⌜*Lucentio exits with Bianca.*⌝
BIONDELLO Nay, faith, I'll see the church a' your back, 5
and then come back to my ⌜master's⌝ as soon as I
can.   ⌜*He exits.*⌝
GREMIO I marvel Cambio comes not all this while.

Enter Petruchio, Katherine, Vincentio, Grumio, with
Attendants.

PETRUCHIO
Sir, here's the door. This is Lucentio's house.
My father's bears more toward the marketplace. 10
Thither must I, and here I leave you, sir.
VINCENTIO
You shall not choose but drink before you go.
I think I shall command your welcome here,
And by all likelihood some cheer is toward.
⌜*He*⌝ *knocks.*

195

20, 22. withal: i.e., with

28. frivolous circumstances: i.e., silly details

38. flat: downright

41. cosen: cheat

42. under my countenance: i.e., by exploiting my good name

44. good shipping: i.e., good luck

GREMIO, ⌜*coming forward*⌝
  They're busy within. You were best knock louder.   15
          ⌜*Merchant*⌝ *looks out of the window.*
⌜MERCHANT, *as* VINCENTIO⌝ What's he that knocks as
  he would beat down the gate?
VINCENTIO Is Signior Lucentio within, sir?
⌜MERCHANT, *as* VINCENTIO⌝ He's within, sir, but not to
  be spoken withal.   20
VINCENTIO What if a man bring him a hundred pound
  or two to make merry withal?
⌜MERCHANT, *as* VINCENTIO⌝ Keep your hundred
  pounds to yourself. He shall need none so long as I
  live.   25
PETRUCHIO, ⌜*to Vincentio*⌝ Nay, I told you your son was
  well beloved in Padua.—Do you hear, sir? To leave
  frivolous circumstances, I pray you tell Signior
  Lucentio that his father is come from Pisa and is
  here at the door to speak with him.   30
⌜MERCHANT, *as* VINCENTIO⌝ Thou liest. His father is
  come from Padua and here looking out at the
  window.
VINCENTIO Art thou his father?
⌜MERCHANT, *as* VINCENTIO⌝ Ay, sir, so his mother says,   35
  if I may believe her.
PETRUCHIO, ⌜*to Vincentio*⌝ Why, how now, gentleman!
  Why, this is flat knavery, to take upon you another
  man's name.
⌜MERCHANT, *as* VINCENTIO⌝ Lay hands on the villain. I   40
  believe he means to cosen somebody in this city
  under my countenance.

          Enter Biondello.

BIONDELLO, ⌜*aside*⌝ I have seen them in the church
  together. God send 'em good shipping! But who is
  here? Mine old master Vincentio! Now we are   45
  undone and brought to nothing.

47. **crack-hemp:** i.e., rogue (literally, someone who will stretch the hangman's rope)

48. **I may choose:** i.e., go my own way

67. **fine villain:** splendidly dressed rogue; **doublet:** jacket

68. **hose:** breeches; **copatain:** high-crowned

69. **undone:** ruined, destroyed

69–70. **play the good husband:** i.e., conserve, save money

75. **habit:** clothes

76. **'cerns:** i.e., concerns

78. **maintain:** afford

VINCENTIO, ⌐*to Biondello*⌐   Come hither, crack-hemp.

BIONDELLO   I hope I may choose, sir.

VINCENTIO   Come hither, you rogue! What, have you
forgot me?   50

BIONDELLO   Forgot you? No, sir. I could not forget you,
for I never saw you before in all my life.

VINCENTIO   What, you notorious villain, didst thou
never see thy ⌐master's⌐ father, Vincentio?

BIONDELLO   What, my old worshipful old master? Yes,   55
marry, sir. See where he looks out of the window.

VINCENTIO   Is't so indeed?   *He beats Biondello.*

BIONDELLO   Help, help, help! Here's a madman will
murder me.   ⌐*Biondello exits.*⌐

⌐MERCHANT, *as* VINCENTIO⌐   Help, son! Help, Signior   60
Baptista!   ⌐*He exits from window.*⌐

PETRUCHIO   Prithee, Kate, let's stand aside and see the
end of this controversy.   ⌐*They move aside.*⌐

Enter ⌐*Merchant*⌐ *with Servants,* ⌐*and*⌐ *Baptista* ⌐*and*⌐
Tranio ⌐*disguised as Lucentio.*⌐

TRANIO, ⌐*as* LUCENTIO⌐   Sir, what are you that offer to
beat my servant?   65

VINCENTIO   What am I, sir? Nay, what are you, sir! O
immortal gods! O fine villain! A silken doublet, a
velvet hose, a scarlet cloak, and a copatain hat! O, I
am undone, I am undone! While I play the good
husband at home, my son and my servant spend all   70
at the university.

TRANIO, ⌐*as* LUCENTIO⌐   How now, what's the matter?

BAPTISTA   What, is the man lunatic?

TRANIO, ⌐*as* LUCENTIO⌐   Sir, you seem a sober ancient
gentleman by your habit, but your words show you   75
a madman. Why, sir, what 'cerns it you if I wear
pearl and gold? I thank my good father, I am able
to maintain it.

82. **his name:** i.e., Tranio's name
95. **forthcoming:** produced (at the time of his trial)
100-1. **cony-catched:** deceived and victimized
102. **right:** true
108. **dotard:** foolish old man
109. **haled:** molested

VINCENTIO   Thy father! O villain, he is a sailmaker in
Bergamo.   80
BAPTISTA   You mistake, sir, you mistake, sir! Pray, what
do you think is his name?
VINCENTIO   His name? As if I knew not his name! I have
brought him up ever since he was three years old,
and his name is Tranio.   85
⌜MERCHANT, *as* VINCENTIO⌝   Away, away, mad ass! His
name is Lucentio and he is mine only son, and heir
to the lands of me, Signior Vincentio.
VINCENTIO   Lucentio? O, he hath murdered his master!
Lay hold on him, I charge you in the Duke's name.   90
O, my son, my son! Tell me, thou villain, where is
my son Lucentio?
TRANIO, ⌜*as* LUCENTIO⌝   Call forth an officer.

⌜*Enter an Officer.*⌝

Carry this mad knave to the jail.—Father Baptista, I
charge you see that he be forthcoming.   95
VINCENTIO   Carry me to the jail?
GREMIO   Stay, officer. He shall not go to prison.
BAPTISTA   Talk not, Signior Gremio. I say he shall go to
prison.
GREMIO   Take heed, Signior Baptista, lest you be cony-   100
catched in this business. I dare swear this is the
right Vincentio.
⌜MERCHANT, *as* VINCENTIO⌝   Swear, if thou dar'st.
GREMIO   Nay, I dare not swear it.
TRANIO, ⌜*as* LUCENTIO⌝   Then thou wert best say that I   105
am not Lucentio.
GREMIO   Yes, I know thee to be Signior Lucentio.
BAPTISTA   Away with the dotard, to the jail with him.
VINCENTIO   Thus strangers may be haled and abused.—
O monstrous villain!   110

Enter Biondello, Lucentio and Bianca.

201

111. **spoiled:** ruined
119. **Right:** true
121. **counterfeit supposes:** false impersonations; **eyne:** i.e., eyes
122. **packing:** plotting, conspiracy; **with a witness:** i.e., with a vengeance
124. **faced and braved:** i.e., defied
128. **state:** status
129. **countenance:** i.e., position and reputation
131. **Unto:** i.e., at

BIONDELLO   O, we are spoiled, and yonder he is! Deny
   him, forswear him, or else we are all undone.
                Biondello, Tranio, and ⌈Merchant⌉
                     exit as fast as may be.
LUCENTIO
   Pardon, sweet father.   ⌈*Lucentio and Bianca*⌉ *kneel.*
VINCENTIO   Lives my sweet son?
BIANCA
   Pardon, dear father.   115
BAPTISTA   How hast thou offended?
   Where is Lucentio?
LUCENTIO   Here's Lucentio,
   Right son to the right Vincentio,
   That have by marriage made thy daughter mine   120
   While counterfeit supposes bleared thine eyne.
GREMIO
   Here's packing, with a witness, to deceive us all!
VINCENTIO
   Where is that damnèd villain, Tranio,
   That faced and braved me in this matter so?
BAPTISTA
   Why, tell me, is not this my Cambio?   125
BIANCA
   Cambio is changed into Lucentio.
LUCENTIO
   Love wrought these miracles. Bianca's love
   Made me exchange my state with Tranio,
   While he did bear my countenance in the town,
   And happily I have arrivèd at the last   130
   Unto the wishèd haven of my bliss.
   What Tranio did, myself enforced him to.
   Then pardon him, sweet father, for my sake.
VINCENTIO   I'll slit the villain's nose that would have
   sent me to the jail!   135
BAPTISTA   But do you hear, sir, have you married my
   daughter without asking my goodwill?

138–39. **Go to!:** expression of angry impatience

139. **will in:** i.e., will go in

143. **My cake is dough:** proverbial for "I've failed"

144. **Out . . . but:** without hope of anything except

146. **ado:** fuss

156. **Better . . . late:** Petruchio combines two proverbs—"Better once than never" (i.e., "Better late than never") and "It is never too late to mend."

5.2 Three couples attend the wedding banquet—Lucentio and Bianca, Petruchio and Katherine, and Hortensio and the Widow. Petruchio is repeatedly teased about being married to a shrew. In retaliation Petruchio wagers with Lucentio and Hortensio that if they all summon their wives to them, his Katherine will be the most obedient in responding. When Bianca and the Widow refuse to come at all and Katherine promptly appears, Petruchio wins, and then he sends Katherine to bring the other wives to their husbands. When they return, Petruchio tells Katherine to instruct the other wives in their wifely duty. Katherine delivers a long speech in praise of women's submission to their husbands. Petruchio kisses Katherine, and they go off to bed.

0 SD. **banquet:** dessert and wine

1. **At last, though long:** i.e., at long last

VINCENTIO   Fear not, Baptista, we will content you. Go
to! But I will in to be revenged for this villainy.
He exits.

BAPTISTA   And I to sound the depth of this knavery.   140
He exits.

LUCENTIO   Look not pale, Bianca. Thy father will not
frown.   *They exit.*

GREMIO
My cake is dough, but I'll in among the rest,
Out of hope of all but my share of the feast.
⌜*He exits.*⌝

KATHERINE   Husband, let's follow to see the end of   145
this ado.

PETRUCHIO   First kiss me, Kate, and we will.

KATHERINE   What, in the midst of the street?

PETRUCHIO   What, art thou ashamed of me?

KATHERINE   ⌜No,⌝ sir, God forbid, but ashamed to kiss.   150

PETRUCHIO
Why, then, let's home again. ⌜*To Grumio.*⌝ Come,
sirrah, let's away.

KATHERINE
Nay, I will give thee a kiss.   ⌜*She kisses him.*⌝
Now pray thee, love, stay.

PETRUCHIO
Is not this well? Come, my sweet Kate.   155
Better once than never, for never too late.
They exit.

⌜Scene 2⌝
Enter Baptista, Vincentio, Gremio, the ⌜*Merchant,*⌝
Lucentio, and Bianca; ⌜*Hortensio*⌝ *and* ⌜*the*⌝ *Widow,*
⌜*Petruchio and Katherine;*⌝ *Tranio, Biondello,* ⌜*and*⌝
Grumio, ⌜*with*⌝ *Servingmen bringing in a banquet.*

LUCENTIO
At last, though long, our jarring notes agree,

3. **'scapes:** i.e., escapes; **overblown:** i.e., past

10. **great good cheer:** i.e., the wedding feast

15. **would:** wish

16. **fears:** is afraid of (She takes **fears** to mean "frightens.")

17. **afeard:** afraid

21. **Roundly:** bluntly

23. **Thus I conceive by him:** i.e., I come to this understanding through observing him

And time it is when raging war is ⌜done⌝
To smile at 'scapes and perils overblown.
My fair Bianca, bid my father welcome,
While I with selfsame kindness welcome thine.   5
Brother Petruchio, sister Katherina,
And thou, Hortensio, with thy loving widow,
Feast with the best, and welcome to my house.
My banquet is to close our stomachs up
After our great good cheer. Pray you, sit down,   10
For now we sit to chat as well as eat.   ⌜*They sit.*⌝

PETRUCHIO
Nothing but sit and sit, and eat and eat!

BAPTISTA
Padua affords this kindness, son Petruchio.

PETRUCHIO
Padua affords nothing but what is kind.

HORTENSIO
For both our sakes I would that word were true.   15

PETRUCHIO
Now, for my life, Hortensio fears his widow!

WIDOW
Then never trust me if I be afeard.

PETRUCHIO
You are very sensible, and yet you miss my sense:
I mean Hortensio is afeard of you.

WIDOW
He that is giddy thinks the world turns round.   20

PETRUCHIO
Roundly replied.

KATHERINE   Mistress, how mean you that?

WIDOW   Thus I conceive by him.

PETRUCHIO
Conceives by me? How likes Hortensio that?

HORTENSIO
My widow says, thus she conceives her tale.   25

207

30. **his:** i.e., his own (Petruchio's)

34. **mean . . . you:** (1) temperate compared to you; (2) nasty, where you are concerned

37. **marks:** i.e., coins (A "mark" was worth 13 shillings.); **put her down:** defeat her

38. **office:** duty, privilege (Hortensio takes "put her down" in the sexual sense.)

39. **Ha' to:** i.e., here's to

41. **butt together:** knock heads

42. **body:** i.e., person

43. **horn:** symbol of a cuckold

47. **Have at you for:** i.e., I challenge you to

PETRUCHIO
  Very well mended. Kiss him for that, good widow.
KATHERINE
  "He that is giddy thinks the world turns round"—
  I pray you tell me what you meant by that.
WIDOW
  Your husband being troubled with a shrew
  Measures my husband's sorrow by his woe.   30
  And now you know my meaning.
KATHERINE
  A very mean meaning.
WIDOW   Right, I mean you.
KATHERINE
  And I am mean indeed, respecting you.
PETRUCHIO   To her, Kate!   35
HORTENSIO   To her, widow!
PETRUCHIO
  A hundred marks, my Kate does put her down.
HORTENSIO   That's my office.
PETRUCHIO
  Spoke like an officer! Ha' to thee, lad.
                        ⌜He⌝ drinks to Hortensio.
BAPTISTA
  How likes Gremio these quick-witted folks?   40
GREMIO
  Believe me, sir, they butt together well.
BIANCA
  Head and butt! An hasty-witted body
  Would say your head and butt were head and horn.
VINCENTIO
  Ay, mistress bride, hath that awakened you?
BIANCA
  Ay, but not frighted me. Therefore I'll sleep again.   45
PETRUCHIO
  Nay, that you shall not. Since you have begun,
  Have at you for a ⌜bitter⌝ jest or two.

209

48. **bird:** i.e., target
51. **prevented me:** stopped me in advance
53. **health:** toast
54. **slipped:** loosed
56. **something:** i.e., somewhat
58. **deer . . . bay:** The image is perhaps of the cornered animal defending itself against the attacking hounds; or, perhaps, Tranio is picturing Kate as a deer cornering the hunter.
60. **gird:** biting remark
62. **galled:** scratched, irritated
65. **in good sadness:** i.e., seriously
66. **veriest shrew:** i.e., shrew in the truest sense, the most complete shrew
67. **for assurance:** i.e., to put it to the test

BIANCA

   Am I your bird? I mean to shift my bush,
   And then pursue me as you draw your bow.—
   You are welcome all.   50

                Bianca, ⌜Katherine, and the Widow⌝ exit.

PETRUCHIO

   She hath prevented me. Here, Signior Tranio,
   This bird you aimed at, though you hit her not.—
   Therefore a health to all that shot and missed.

TRANIO

   O, sir, Lucentio slipped me like his greyhound,
   Which runs himself and catches for his master.   55

PETRUCHIO

   A good swift simile, but something currish.

TRANIO

   'Tis well, sir, that you hunted for yourself.
   'Tis thought your deer does hold you at a bay.

BAPTISTA

   O, O, Petruchio! Tranio hits you now.

LUCENTIO

   I thank thee for that gird, good Tranio.   60

HORTENSIO

   Confess, confess! Hath he not hit you here?

PETRUCHIO

   He has a little galled me, I confess.
   And as the jest did glance away from me,
   'Tis ten to one it maimed you two outright.

BAPTISTA

   Now, in good sadness, son Petruchio,   65
   I think thou hast the veriest shrew of all.

PETRUCHIO

   Well, I say no. And therefore, ⌜for⌝ assurance,
   Let's each one send unto his wife,
   And he whose wife is most obedient
   To come at first when he doth send for her   70
   Shall win the wager which we will propose.

75. **of:** i.e., on
84. **be your half:** assume half your bet
96. **forthwith:** immediately

HORTENSIO
  Content, what's the wager?
LUCENTIO   Twenty crowns.
PETRUCHIO   Twenty crowns?
  I'll venture so much of my hawk or hound,   75
  But twenty times so much upon my wife.
LUCENTIO
  A hundred, then.
HORTENSIO   Content.
PETRUCHIO   A match! 'Tis done.
HORTENSIO   Who shall begin?   80
LUCENTIO   That will I.
  Go, Biondello, bid your mistress come to me.
BIONDELLO   I go.   *He exits.*
BAPTISTA
  Son, I'll be your half Bianca comes.
LUCENTIO
  I'll have no halves. I'll bear it all myself.   85

Enter Biondello

How now, what news?
BIONDELLO   Sir, my mistress sends you
  word
That she is busy, and she cannot come.
PETRUCHIO
  How? "She's busy, and she cannot come"?   90
  Is that an answer?
GREMIO   Ay, and a kind one, too.
  Pray God, sir, your wife send you not a worse.
PETRUCHIO   I hope better.
HORTENSIO
  Sirrah Biondello, go and entreat my wife   95
  To come to me forthwith.   *Biondello exits.*
PETRUCHIO   O ho, entreat her!
  Nay, then, she must needs come.

112. **holidam:** a confusion of "holidom," meaning a relic or the state of holiness, with "holidame," or the Virgin Mary
116. **deny:** i.e., refuse
117. **Swinge me them:** beat them
118. **straight:** immediately
119. **wonder:** miracle
120. **bodes:** foretells, presages

HORTENSIO   I am afraid, sir,
  Do what you can, yours will not be entreated.   100

                    Enter Biondello

  Now, where's my wife?
BIONDELLO
  She says you have some goodly jest in hand.
  She will not come. She bids you come to her.
PETRUCHIO   Worse and worse. She will not come!
  O vile, intolerable, not to be endured!—   105
  Sirrah Grumio, go to your mistress,
  Say I command her come to me.   ⌐*Grumio*⌐ *exits.*
HORTENSIO
  I know her answer.
PETRUCHIO   What?
HORTENSIO   She will not.   110
PETRUCHIO
  The fouler fortune mine, and there an end.

                    Enter Katherine.

BAPTISTA
  Now by my holidam, here comes Katherina!
KATHERINE
  What is your will, sir, that you send for me?
PETRUCHIO
  Where is your sister, and Hortensio's wife?
KATHERINE
  They sit conferring by the parlor fire.   115
PETRUCHIO
  Go fetch them hither. If they deny to come,
  Swinge me them soundly forth unto their husbands.
  Away, I say, and bring them hither straight.
                            ⌐*Katherine exits.*⌐
LUCENTIO
  Here is a wonder, if you talk of a wonder.
HORTENSIO
  And so it is. I wonder what it bodes.   120

122. **awful rule:** rule by commanding respect or awe; **right:** proper

123. **what not:** i.e., anything and everything

124. **fair befall thee:** i.e., good fortune come to you

128. **as:** i.e., as though

132. **froward:** perverse

136. **bauble:** showy trifle

137. **cause:** reason

138. **pass:** state of affairs

139. **duty:** obedience

143. **laying:** betting

PETRUCHIO
Marry, peace it bodes, and love, and quiet life,
An awful rule, and right supremacy,
And, to be short, what not that's sweet and happy.

BAPTISTA
Now fair befall thee, good Petruchio!
The wager thou hast won, and I will add   125
Unto their losses twenty thousand crowns,
Another dowry to another daughter,
For she is changed as she had never been.

PETRUCHIO
Nay, I will win my wager better yet,
And show more sign of her obedience,   130
Her new-built virtue and obedience.

       Enter Katherine, Bianca, and Widow.

See where she comes, and brings your froward
   wives
As prisoners to her womanly persuasion.—
Katherine, that cap of yours becomes you not.   135
Off with that bauble, throw it underfoot.
                 ⌜*She obeys.*⌝

WIDOW
Lord, let me never have a cause to sigh
Till I be brought to such a silly pass.

BIANCA
Fie, what a foolish duty call you this?

LUCENTIO
I would your duty were as foolish too.   140
The wisdom of your duty, fair Bianca,
Hath cost me ⌜a⌝ hundred crowns since suppertime.

BIANCA
The more fool you for laying on my duty.

PETRUCHIO
Katherine, I charge thee tell these headstrong
   women   145
What duty they do owe their lords and husbands.

155. **meads:** meadows

156. **Confounds thy fame:** i.e., spoils your reputation

157. **meet:** appropriate

158. **moved:** angry

159. **ill-seeming:** unbecoming

162–70. **Thy husband . . . debt:** See Paul's *Letter to the Ephesians* 3.22–28 ("Wives, submit yourselves unto your husbands, . . . for the husband is the head of the wife, even as Christ is the head of the Church . . ."). In the Geneva Bible, the marginal gloss adds "So the husband ought to nourish, govern, and defend his wife from perils."

166. **To watch:** i.e., to keep watch throughout

168. **at:** i.e., from

171–76. **Such duty . . . lord:** See 1 Peter 2.13–3.7: "Submit yourselves to every ordinance of man for the Lord's sake: whether it be to the king . . . or unto governors. . . . Likewise, ye wives, be in subjection to your own husbands. . . ."

177. **simple:** foolish

WIDOW
  Come, come, ⌈you're⌉ mocking. We will have no
    telling.
PETRUCHIO
  Come on, I say, and first begin with her.
WIDOW She shall not.   150
PETRUCHIO
  I say she shall.—And first begin with her.
KATHERINE
  Fie, fie! Unknit that threat'ning unkind brow,
  And dart not scornful glances from those eyes
  To wound thy lord, thy king, thy governor.
  It blots thy beauty as frosts do bite the meads,   155
  Confounds thy fame as whirlwinds shake fair buds,
  And in no sense is meet or amiable.
  A woman moved is like a fountain troubled,
  Muddy, ill-seeming, thick, bereft of beauty,
  And while it is so, none so dry or thirsty   160
  Will deign to sip or touch one drop of it.
  Thy husband is thy lord, thy life, thy keeper,
  Thy head, thy sovereign, one that cares for thee,
  And for thy maintenance commits his body
  To painful labor both by sea and land,   165
  To watch the night in storms, the day in cold,
  Whilst thou liest warm at home, secure and safe,
  And craves no other tribute at thy hands
  But love, fair looks, and true obedience—
  Too little payment for so great a debt.   170
  Such duty as the subject owes the prince,
  Even such a woman oweth to her husband;
  And when she is froward, peevish, sullen, sour,
  And not obedient to his honest will,
  What is she but a foul contending rebel   175
  And graceless traitor to her loving lord?
  I am ashamed that women are so simple
  To offer war where they should kneel for peace,

179. **sway:** power
182. **Unapt:** unsuited
183. **conditions:** qualities
185. **unable:** helpless
186. **big:** self-important
187. **heart:** courage
188. **bandy:** exchange; literally, hit back and forth
190. **as weak:** i.e., as weak as straws; **past compare:** beyond comparison
192. **vail your stomachs:** i.e., subdue your pride; **no boot:** i.e., bootless, futile
195. **may it:** i.e., if it may
197. **ha 't:** have it (i.e., you win)
198. **a good hearing:** i.e., good to hear; **toward:** compliant, cooperative
201. **We three:** i.e., Petruchio, Hortensio, Lucentio; **sped:** done for
203. **the white:** the bull's eye (i.e., won the woman prized by all, Bianca, whose name in Italian means "white")
204. **God:** i.e., I pray God to

Hitting "the white." (5.2.203)
From Gilles Corrozet, *Hecatongraphie* . . . (1543).

Or seek for rule, supremacy, and sway
When they are bound to serve, love, and obey.   180
Why are our bodies soft and weak and smooth,
Unapt to toil and trouble in the world,
But that our soft conditions and our hearts
Should well agree with our external parts?
Come, come, you froward and unable worms!   185
My mind hath been as big as one of yours,
My heart as great, my reason haply more,
To bandy word for word and frown for frown;
But now I see our lances are but straws,
Our strength as weak, our weakness past compare,   190
That seeming to be most which we indeed least are.
Then vail your stomachs, for it is no boot,
And place your hands below your husband's foot;
In token of which duty, if he please,
My hand is ready, may it do him ease.   195

PETRUCHIO
Why, there's a wench! Come on, and kiss me, Kate.
                                        ⌐*They kiss.*⌐

LUCENTIO
Well, go thy ways, old lad, for thou shalt ha 't.

VINCENTIO
'Tis a good hearing when children are toward.

LUCENTIO
But a harsh hearing when women are froward.

PETRUCHIO   Come, Kate, we'll to bed.   200
We three are married, but you two are sped.
⌐*To Lucentio.*⌐ 'Twas I won the wager, though you
     hit the white,
And being a winner, God give you good night.
                         Petruchio ⌐*and Katherine*⌐ *exit.*

HORTENSIO
Now, go thy ways, thou hast tamed a curst shrow.   205

LUCENTIO
'Tis a wonder, by your leave, she will be tamed so.
                                        ⌐*They exit.*⌐

221

Textual Notes

The reading of the present text appears to the left of the square bracket. The earliest sources of readings not in F, the First Folio text (upon which this edition is based), are indicated as follows: **Q** is *The Taming of a Shrew* 1594; **F2** is the Second Folio of 1632; **F3** is the Third Folio of 1663–64; **F4** is the Fourth Folio of 1685. **Ed.** is an earlier editor of Shakespeare, beginning with Rowe in 1709. No sources are given for emendations of punctuation or for corrections of obvious typographical errors, like turned letters that produce no known word. **SD** means stage direction; **SP** means speech prefix; **uncorr.** means the first or uncorrected state of the First Folio; **corr.** means the second or corrected state of the First Folio; ~ stands in place of a word already quoted before the square bracket; ʌ indicates the omission of a punctuation mark.

Ind.1] Ed.; *Actus primus. Scœna Prima.* F

Ind.1   0. SD *Enter Begger and Hostes, Christophero Sly.* F

1. SP SLY] Ed.; *Begger* F

3 *and hereafter* SP SLY] Ed.; *Beg.* F

9. Saint] Ed.; *S.* F

17. Breathe] Ed.; *Brach* F

22, 30. SP FIRST HUNTSMAN] Ed.; *Hunts.* F

44. SP THIRD HUNTSMAN] This ed.; *1. Hun.* F

72. SP THIRD HUNTSMAN] This ed.; *1. Hunts.* F

83. SD *1 line earlier in* F

87. SP FIRST PLAYER] Ed.; *2. Player* F

93. SP SECOND PLAYER] Ed.; *Sincklo* (*the name of an actor in Shakespeare's company*) F

105. SP FIRST PLAYER] Ed.; *Plai.* F

Ind.2 18. Sly's] Ed.; Sies F
26 *and hereafter* SP SERVINGMAN] Ed.; *Man.*
  (*man.*, *M.*) F
94. Greete] Ed.; Greece F
100. SD *1 line earlier in* F
111. Alice] *Alce* F
139–40. I will. Let them play it. Is not] I will let
  them play, it is not F
144. a] a a F

1.1 0. SD *Tranio*] *Triano* F
13. Vincentio] Ed.; *Vincentio's* F
14. brought] brough F
17–18. study ˏ / Virtue] Ed.; ~, / ~ F
25. *Mi perdonato*] Ed.; *Me Pardonato* F
33. Ovid ˏ] ~; F
45. SD *2 lines later in* F
45. SD *suitors*] This ed.; *sister* F; *suitor* F2
92. resolved] resould F
147. SD *Gremio . . . onstage.*] *Exeunt ambo.*
  Manet Tranio and Lucentio. F
164. *captum*] F2; *captam* F
213. colored] Conlord F
242. Ay, sir] Ed.; I sir F
254. your] F2; you F
258. SD *speak*] Ed.; *speakes* F

1.2 26. *Con tutto il cuore ben trovato*] Ed.;
  Contutti le core bene trobatto F
27. *ben*] Ed.; *bene* F
27. *molto*] Ed.; *multo* F
28. *honorato*] Ed.; *honorata* F
28. *signor*] Ed.; *signior* F
47. 'twixt] twixr F
53. grows. But . . . few,] ~ ˏ ~ . . . ~. F
74. me, were] ~. ~ F
74. she as] Ed.; she is as F
122. me and other] Ed.; me. Other F

140. SD 2 *lines earlier in* F
140. SD *disguised*] *disgused* F
174. me] Ed.; one F
186. dowry] F (corr.); dowric F (uncorr.)
192. Antonio's] *Butonios* F
221. SD *disguised as Lucentio*] Ed.; *braue* F
229. sir] F (corr.); fir F (ucorr.)
237. streets] streers F
260. The] F (corr.); Tne F (uncorr.)
269. first] F (corr.); sirst F (uncorr.)
273. feat] Ed.; seeke F
288. *ben*] F2; *Been* F
2.1   8. thee] F2; *omit* F
  21. SD *1 line earlier in* F
79–80. wooing. Neighbor, this] Ed.; wooing neighbors: this F
  83. you] Ed.; *omit* F
  95. a suitor] as utor F
109. Pisa. By] Ed.; ~ ‸ ~ F
176. SD *1 line earlier in* F
262. askance] Ed.; a sconce F
270. than] rhen F
293. SD *3 lines earlier in* F
293. SD *Tranio*] *Trayno* F
320. goodnight] godnight F
349. in] Ed.; me F
422. SD *1 line earlier in* F
3.1   30. *hic*] *hie* F
30, 35, 45. *Sigeia*] F2; *sigeria* F
  46. *steterat*] F2; *staterat* F
  51. SP How] Ed.; *Luc.* How F
  54. SP BIANCA In] Ed.; In F
  55. SP LUCENTIO] Ed.; *Bian.* F
  57. SP BIANCA] Ed.; *Hort.* F
  77. *A re*] Q; *Are* F
  78. *B mi*] Ed.; *Beeme* F

	79. *C fa ut*] Q; *C favt* F
	84. change] F2; charge F
	84. odd] Ed.; old F
	84. SD *Servant*] Ed.; *Messenger* F
	85. SP SERVANT] Ed.; *Nicke.* F
3.2	14. man,] ~; F
	29. thy] F2; *omit* F
	30. old] Ed.; *omit* F
	33. hear] Q; heard F
	54. swayed] Ed.; Waid F
	129. SD *Exit.* F
	130. to] Ed.; *omit* F
	132. I] F2; *omit* F
	155. grumbling] grumlling F
	184. SD *1 line later in* F
	202. SP GREMIO] F2; *Gra.* F
4.1	24. SP CURTIS] Q; *Gru.* F
	45. their] F3; the F
	98. SD *1 line earlier in* F
	110. SP GRUMIO] F3; *Gre.* F
	180. SD *Enter Curtis*] *Enter Curtis a Seruant.* F, *1 line later*
4.2	4. SP HORTENSIO] F2; *Luc.* F
	6. SP LUCENTIO] F2; *Hor.* F
	7. you? First . . . that.] Ed.; ~ ʌ ~ . . . ~? F
	8. SP LUCENTIO] F2; *Hor.* F
	8. profess,] ~ ʌ F
	10. prove] ptoue F
	13. none] Ed.; me F
	31. her] F3; them F
	35. forsworn!] ~ ʌ F
	68. countenance] eountenance F
	72. Minola ʌ] ~. F
	74. Take] F2; *Par.* Take F
	74. in] Ed.; me F
	74 SD *and hereafter Merchant*] Ed.; *Pedant* F (*Ped.* in SP's)

4.3	0.4.3] Ed.; *Actus Quartus, Scena Prima.* F
	65. SD *1 line earlier in* F
	67. SP HABERDASHER] Ed.; *Fel.* F
	86. a] Q; *omit* F
	93. a] Q; *omit* F
	115. yard,] ~ ⌃ F
	187. account'st] Ed.; accountedst F
	195. And] Aud F
4.4	0. SD *booted, and*] F *at line 19* SD *repeats the Pedant-Merchant's entrance:* "Enter . . . Pedant booted and bare headed."
	1. Sir] Ed.; Sirs F
	4. Genoa,] ~. F
	5. Where] Ed.; *Tra.* Where F
	8. SD *1 line earlier in* F
	18. SD *1 line later in* F
	19. SD *See note to 4.4.0 SD.*
	67. SD *Exit.* F *1 line later*
	69. SD *Enter Peter.* F
	73. SD *Enter Lucentio.*] Ed.; *Enter Lucentio and Biondello.* F
	92. except] F2; expect F
	97. for] fot F
4.5	21. is] Q; in F
	42. where] F2; whether F
	45. Allots] Q; A lots F
	83. be] F2; *omit* F
5.1	0. SD *Bianca*] *Bianea* F
	4. SD *Exit.* F
	6. master's] Ed.; Mistris F
	14. SD *He knocks.*] Ed.; *Knock.* F
	46. brought] brough F
	54. master's] F2; Mistris F
	67. doublet] doubtlet F
	85. Tranio] Tronio F
	110. SD *2 lines earlier in* F
	110. SD *Bianca*] *Biancu* F

125. SP BAPTISTA] *Bvp.* F
143. dough, but] doug, hbut F
150. No] Mo F
156. never,] ueuer, F

5.2   0.5.2] Ed.; *Actus Quintus* F
0. SD *Enter Baptista, Vincentio, Gremio, the Pedant, Lucentio, and Bianca. Tranio, Biondello Grumio, and Widdow: The Seruingmen with Tranio bringing in a Banquet.* F
2. done] Ed.; come F
39. thee] F (the)
42. butt!] ~ ˌ F
47. bitter] Ed.; better F
54. SP TRANIO] *Tri.* F
64. two] F (too)
67. for] F2; sir F
100. SD *1/2 line earlier in* F
142. a] Ed.; fiue F
147. you're] F3; your F
152. threat'ning] thretaning F
164. maintenanceˌ]~. F
200. we'll] weee'le F

The Taming of the Shrew:
A Modern Perspective

Karen Newman

In sermons preached from the pulpit, in exhortations urged from the magistrate's bench, in plays and popular pastimes, in morning and evening prayers at home, in early printed books rehearsing seemly female conduct, the tripartite ideal of women's chastity, silence, and obedience was proclaimed far and wide in early modern England. Shakespeare's heroine, Kate, in *The Taming of the Shrew* refuses to abide by these Renaissance ideals of womanly submission. Her self-confidence and independence, which the male characters disparage by calling her a "devil," threaten the hierarchical organization of Renaissance society in which women were believed inferior. The price of Kate's resistance is summed up in Hortensio's taunt, "No mates for you, / Unless you were of gentler, milder mold."

Instead of wooing Kate, the suitors pursue her more tractable sister, Bianca, whom they admire for her silence, mildness, and sobriety. But in Bianca's dealings with her two suitors (disguised as tutors), even Bianca shows herself less docile than she seems. As many readers of *The Taming of the Shrew* have noted, if in the end one shrew is tamed, two more reveal themselves: Bianca and the widow refuse to do their husbands' bidding at the very moment Kate has ostensibly learned to obey. In the play, the gulf between Renaissance ideals of a submissive femininity and the realities of women's behavior is wide.

Recently, commentators have turned to the work of

social historians to explain *The Taming of the Shrew*'s presentation of the female characters' transgression of Renaissance standards for women's behavior. They point out that during the period from 1560 until the English civil war, England suffered a "crisis of order" brought about by enormous economic, demographic, and political changes that produced acute anxiety about conventional hierarchies.[1] Groups that had traditionally been subject to the authority of others—merchants and actors, servants and apprentices—were enabled by rapid change to enter social spheres that had been customarily closed to them. Such shifts threatened perceived hierarchies in Tudor and Stuart England: men complained of upstart courtiership, of a socially mobile middle class, of "masterless men," and of female rebellion. Since public and domestic authority in Elizabethan England was vested in men—in fathers, husbands, masters, teachers, magistrates, lords—Elizabeth I's rule inevitably produced anxiety about women's roles.[2]

Arraignments for scolding, shrewishness, and bastardy, as well as witchcraft persecutions, crowd the historical record.[3] Although men were occasionally charged with scolding, shrewishness was a predominately female offense. Punishment for such crimes and for related offenses involving sexual misbehavior or "domineering" wives who "beat" or "abused" their husbands often involved public humiliation: the ducking stool, "carting," and/or reproof by means of the skymmington or charivari (an informal ritual in which the accused woman or her surrogate was put in a scold's collar or paraded through the village or town in a cart accompanied by a procession of neighbors banging pots and pans). In Shakespeare's play we can observe traces of such practices when Baptista, Kate's father, exhorts Bianca's suitors to court Kate instead and Gremio exclaims, "To cart her, rather. She's too rough for me."

Anxiety about changing social relations prompted the labeling of old behaviors in new ways that made criminals of women whose actions threatened patriarchal authority.

But history alone cannot account for Shakespeare's presentation of the shrew-taming plot. Literary history —generic models and conventions, both popular and elite—shaped the way Shakespeare represents the play's characters and action. Popular medieval *fabliaux* and Tudor jest books and pamphlets recount tales of shrew-taming that furnished patterns from which Shakespeare drew. These and the oral folktales on which they are based include incidents similar to the plot of *The Taming of the Shrew*: a father with two daughters, one curst (i.e., bad-tempered) and spurned, the other mild and sought after; a suitor determined to tame the shrew; a farcical wedding scene; quarrels of the sort Kate and Petruchio have at his country house and on the road to Padua, and a bet on the most obedient wife. An often-cited example is the anonymous *A Merry Jest of a Shrewd and Curst Wife Lapped in Morel's Skin for her Good Behavior* (c. 1550) in which a father has two daughters, one curst, the other docile. When a wooer seeks the shrewish daughter's hand, the father warns him against this "devilish fiend of hell." Unmoved, he marries her and proceeds to tame her by means of beatings and torture: after cudgeling her bloody, he wraps her in a salted morel skin. The ballad ends conventionally with a meal at which father, mother, and neighbors admire the once-shrewish wife's obedience and with a challenge to the audience: "He that can charm a shrewd wife / Better than thus, Let him come to me and fetch ten pound / And a golden purse."

Though the basic situation of *The Taming of the Shrew* resembles that of *A Merry Jest*, in Shakespeare's play Petruchio avoids physical violence. Instead of beating Kate, he resorts to more civilized coercion: public

humiliation at their wedding, starvation, sleep depriva-
tion, and verbal bullying, all administered with the
utmost courtesy and pretended kindness. The less violent but equally coercive taming strategies that Shakespeare has Petruchio employ can be linked to a humanist tradition represented by Juan Luis Vives, Erasmus,
and later Protestant reformers, who recommend persuasion, not brutality, as the means of inculcating wifely
obedience. But even the popular tradition offers ana-
logues less grisly than *A Merry Jest*. For example, in the
early broadside, *The Taming of a Shrew or the only way to
make a Bad Wife Good: At least, to keep her quiet, be she
bad or good*, a father counsels his newly married son not
to chide his wife and to give her reign over the household to prevent marital strife.

In both popular and elite materials on marriage and
education, taming or educating a wife is likened to
the training or domestication of animals—unbroken
horses, untractable cats, untamed hawks, even wild
beasts. Implied in this comparison is the view that
women are themselves unmanageable creatures whom
only rigorous training and violence, or the continued
threat of violence, can render submissive. Popular folktales and *fabliaux*, marital handbooks, sermons, and
educational treatises all resort to the language and
vocabularies of animal taming. In *The Taming of the
Shrew*, Shakespeare has Petruchio compare taming
Kate to training a falcon, and he peppers Petruchio's
speech with the technical language of hawk taming.

The humanist writers also sought to inculcate obedience through a less dehumanizing but perhaps more
powerfully manipulative method. Following such earlier
writers as Saint Paul, they set up an analogy in which
marriage and the family are likened to the government
of the kingdom. The family is represented as a little
world organized like the larger world of the state or

commonwealth, and the wife's duty to obey her husband is equated with the subject's duty to obey the prince. Wifely obedience, according to this model, is exacted not through violence but through strategies of molding the wife into a fit subject. In early modern England, the family was the basic unit of production as well as consumption, the site of the pooling and distribution of resources and of the reproduction of proper subjects for the commonwealth. In such a world, managing femininity had important political as well as social and economic consequences: in Elizabethan England a woman who murdered her spouse was tried not for murder as was her male counterpart but for treason, and her punishment was correspondingly more severe.

Kate's speech at the end of the play on the status of wives as subjects most forcefully illustrates this rationalization of wifely subjection:

> Such duty as the subject owes the prince,
> Even such a woman oweth to her husband;
> And when she is froward, peevish, sullen, sour,
> And not obedient to his honest will,
> What is she but a foul contending rebel
> And graceless traitor to her loving lord?
>
> (5.2.171–76)

No lines in the play have been more variously interpreted than this final speech in which Kate advocates women's submission to their husbands' wills. Some critics have accepted Kate's speech simply as testimony that she has been tamed; others argue that it must be understood ironically as pretense, a strategy for living peaceably in patriarchal culture. Although either interpretation can be supported by the text and by a director's choices in the theater, what is perhaps most striking about Kate's final speech is that at the very moment the ideology of women's silence and submission is most forcefully articulated, we find a woman (or at any rate, a boy playing a woman's part, since on the Elizabethan stage all women's parts were played by boy actors) speaking forcefully and in public the longest speech in the play, at the most dramatic moment in the action. In short, Kate's speaking as she does contradicts the very sentiments she affirms.

Not only does Shakespeare's shrew-taming plot depend on generic models—*fabliaux*, folktales, educational treatises, sermons and the like—but the subplot—the wooing of Bianca—also depends on literary models, in particular George Gascoigne's *Supposes* (1566), a translation of the Italian comedy *I Suppositi* (1509) by the Italian poet and playwright Lodovico Ariosto (1474–1533). Ariosto's play was modeled on the classical new comic tradition generally traced to the Greek playwright Menander (4th century B.C.) and made available to the Renaissance through his Latin imitators Plautus (254?–184 B.C.) and Terence (185–159 B.C.).[4] Typically, the plot structure of new comedy involves young people whose desire for one another is opposed by the young man's father, or by a pimp, or by some other representative of an older generation. The plot depends on a trick or twist usually involving money and perpetrated by a servant or slave that allows the lovers to be united. In the Greco-Roman tradition, the female character is often an unmarriageable slave or courtesan, and the resolution sometimes entails mistaken identity—the woman is discovered to be a citizen lost or sold into slavery at birth, in which case the play can end in marriage.

Early Renaissance versions of such comedies transform the social and sexual relations typical of new-comic plots: the young woman is typically marriageable, the opposition is often her father, and the sexual intrigue usually ends in marriage. Shakespeare and the

English playwrights modify this structure further by melding it with the romance tradition of the chaste lover (like Lucentio) who wishes only for marriage from the start. In addition, in *The Taming of the Shrew* Shakespeare adds a rival for Bianca's hand (Hortensio) to enhance the romantic plot by allowing her a choice between possible husbands. New comedy typically follows the unities of time and place: the lovers are already at odds with some authority at the outset, and the play enacts only the intrigue that brings them together. Shakespeare, however, dramatizes the entire action, from Lucentio's falling in love and wooing Bianca through the intrigue that leads to their marriage and on to the celebratory feast at the end.

In *The Taming of the Shrew*, Shakespeare carefully interweaves his main plot and his subplot: Lucentio sees and loves Bianca (1.1); Petruchio vows to marry Kate (1.2); Petruchio woos her (2.1); Lucentio and Hortensio woo Bianca (3.1). The plots diverge at the marriage of Kate and Petruchio (3.2), briefly to reunite (after the taming scenes at Petruchio's house and Lucentio's gulling of Baptista) on the journey back to Padua when Kate calls Lucentio's father a "young budding virgin." That "mistaken" identity in turn prepares for another, Tranio's refusal to recognize Vincentio in 5.1, a complication resolved by the appearance of the young lovers as husband and wife. The two plots are united again in the conventional comic feast and wager that end the play.

The convention of mistaken identity, which Shakespeare inherited from his classical and Italian predecessors, is not only a plot device in the play, but also works thematically to undermine notions of an essential self or a fixed identity. In the Induction (an eighteenth-century editorial appellation, since the Sly incidents are simply part of Act 1 in the First Folio [1623], the earliest printed edition of *The Taming of the Shrew*), Sly is persuaded he is a lord instead of a tinker; in the opening scene of the play proper, Lucentio and Tranio exchange identities as master and servant. Kate is transformed after enduring the irrational world of Petruchio's country house, where she is denied food, sleep, and the fashionable accoutrements of her social class until

> . . . she (poor soul)
> Knows not which way to stand, to look, to speak,
> And sits as one new-risen from a dream.
> (4.1.184–86)

In the tradition of Shakespeare's later romantic comedies, she subsequently "discovers" a new identity as obedient wife.[5] Bianca and the widow, who begin by conforming to oppressive codes of womanly duty, reveal their independence. The Merchant assumes the identity of Vincentio, while Vincentio is "mistaken" for a "fair lovely maid." Mistaken identity works literally in the disguise plots of the Induction and the Bianca-Lucentio action and figuratively in the taming plot, in which Petruchio plays at antic ruffian and Kate at submissive wife.

The Induction, with its duping of the tinker Sly, is linked to yet another folklore tradition, the motif of the "sleeper awakened" found in many versions throughout the Middle Ages and Renaissance. Usually the story ends with the Sly character returned to his beggarly identity, as in the play published in 1594, the anonymous *A Pleasant Conceited Historie, called The taming of a Shrew,* thought by some to be a poorly transmitted version of Shakespeare's source but believed by others to be based on Shakespeare's play. (See "An Introduction to This Text" for a discussion of the relation of Shakespeare's *The Taming of the Shrew* and the anonymous play.) In the anonymous play, the Sly action is completed with an epilogue in which Sly awakes after the comedy to rediscover himself a tinker and vows to return home to tame his own shrewish wife. Commentators once claimed that Shakespeare concluded his *The Taming of the Shrew* with an epilogue inexplicably omitted from the printed text, but others argue that such a return to the Sly action would have been not only anticlimactic, but technically implausible in light of the Elizabethan theatrical practice of doubling roles with the same actors acting in both Induction and play proper.

The Taming of the Shrew has been popular onstage since its earliest production, though, like many of Shakespeare's plays, in radically altered forms. By the early seventeenth century it had already prompted a sequel, John Fletcher's *The Woman's Prize; or the Tamer Tamed* (c. 1611). In the twentieth century, it has inspired successful musical, popular film, and television adaptations, and numerous stage productions. And the play continues to be a staple in both the secondary and postsecondary school curriculum. The play's contemporary success depends first on comic virtuosity, but in a time of rapid social change when traditional gender roles are being challenged and the malleability of identity is increasingly acknowledged, audiences take pleasure in *The Taming of the Shrew*'s representation of the instability both of conventional gender hierarchies and of human identity itself.

---

1. See particularly Lawrence Stone, *The Causes of the English Revolution 1529–1642* (New York: Harper & Row, 1972) and his *Crisis of the English Aristocracy 1558–1641* (Oxford: Clarendon Press, 1965).

2. On the anxiety produced by Elizabeth, see Louis Montrose, " 'Shaping Fantasies': Gender and Power in Elizabethan Culture," *Representations* 1 (1983): 61–94;

however, see also Leah Marcus, *Puzzling Shakespeare: Local Reading and Its Discontents* (Berkeley: University of California Press, 1988), ch. 2, in which she shows how Elizabeth represented herself as both prince and father to her people.

3. See David Underdown, "The Taming of the Scold: The Enforcement of Patriarchal Authority in Early Modern England," in *Order and Disorder in Early Modern England*, edited by Anthony Fletcher and John Stevenson, pp. 116–35 (Cambridge: Cambridge University Press, 1985).

4. "New" is a misnomer since "new comedy" is dubbed "new" only in relation to the "old" comic tradition represented by Aristophanes (448?–380? B.C.).

5. On Kate's development and *Shrew* as romantic comedy, see John Bean, "Comic Structure and the Humanizing of Kate in *The Taming of the Shrew*," in *The Woman's Part*, edited by Carolyn Ruth Swift Lenz, Gayle Greene, and Carol Thomas Neely, pp. 65–78 (Urbana: University of Illinois Press, 1980).

Further Reading

The Taming of the Shrew

Amussen, Susan. *An Ordered Society: Gender and Class in Early Modern England.* New York: Blackwell, 1988.

Amussen analyzes the hierarchy of class and gender and their often conflictual relationship in the village and family life of early modern England. She focuses on what people in families and villages expected of each other and the underlying assumptions about how their relationships ought to work. The society's organic model of government based upon the family structure began to erode in the early seventeenth century as the first attempts to separate the family from politics took place.

Bean, John C. "Comic Structure and the Humanizing of Kate in *The Taming of the Shrew*." In *The Woman's Part: Feminist Criticism of Shakespeare*, edited by Carolyn Ruth Swift Lenz, Gayle Greene, and Carol Thomas Neely, pp. 65–78. Urbana: University of Illinois Press, 1980.

Bean analyzes the play's contending modes of romance and farce. He defends Kate's final speech as a "humanized vision" of cooperative marriage but argues that the process by which she is brought to make the speech is humiliating and at odds with Shakespeare's attempts to create in Kate a "humanized character." The problem, for Bean, "is not what Kate actually says . . . but the way she is forced by Petruchio to say it."

Belsey, Catherine. "Disrupting Sexual Difference: Meaning and Gender in the Comedies." In *Alternative Shake-*

speares, edited by John Drakakis, pp. 166–90. New York: Methuen, 1985.

Suggesting that Shakespearean comedy can be read as a disruption of sexual difference, Belsey proposes that the comedies call into question "that set of relations between terms which proposes as inevitable an antithesis between masculine and feminine, men and women." For Belsey, the plays provide a site of contest that momentarily unfixes the existing system of differences. In the resulting gap, we can glimpse a mode of being that exists outside sexual stereotyping.

Brunvand, Jan H. "The Folktale Origin of *The Taming of the Shrew.*" *Shakespeare Quarterly* 17 (1966): 345–59.

Brunvand investigates a wealth of folktales sharing the common characteristic of a husband taming a bad wife by "some kind of violent trick." Finding the source for Shakespeare's play in the "circumstantial details and homely spirit of a folktale long mellowed and polished by countless retellings," Brunvand argues that Shakespeare would have been familiar with the tale as it developed through the oral tradition rather than in any literary form.

Bullough, Geoffrey, ed. *Narrative and Dramatic Sources of Shakespeare,* vol. 1, pp. 57–160. New York: Columbia University Press, 1957.

Bullough tracks Shakespeare's many possible sources for *The Taming of the Shrew,* including George Gascoigne's *Supposes* (1566) and an earlier version of *The Shrew* called *The Taming of a Shrew* (1594). The differences between the plays are many, and Bullough argues that "*A Shrew* may not be so much a source play as Shakespeare's first shot at the theme," although the origin of *A Shrew* is in doubt.

"Homily on Obedience" (1559). In *Elizabethan Backgrounds*, edited by Arthur F. Kinney, pp. 44–70. Hamden, Conn.: Archon, 1975.

Read from pulpits throughout the realm, this homily forcefully portrays Elizabethan notions of hierarchy and authority. The sermon emphasizes order through community and hierarchy and warns of the ensuing chaos that would result from individualism.

Kahn, Coppélia. "*The Taming of the Shrew:* Shakespeare's Mirror of Marriage." In *The Authority of Experience*, edited by Arlyn Diamond and Lee Edwards, pp. 84–100. Amherst: University of Massachusetts Press, 1977.

According to Kahn, Shakespeare lived in an age devoted to the "maintenance of order through hierarchy." Petruchio represents this prevailing system of female subjection, his character an exaggerated form of its basic structure. But the myth of female weakness, which assumes that women must submit to man's superior authority, paradoxically reveals a contrary myth: that "only a woman has the power to authenticate a man." That is, Petruchio's authority is ultimately dependent upon Kate.

Newman, Karen. "Renaissance Family Politics and Shakespeare's *The Taming of the Shrew.*" *English Literary Renaissance* 16 (1986): 86–100.

By comparing examples from social history of troubled gender relations with Shakespeare's *Taming of the Shrew*, Newman demonstrates how women were managed in early modern England. Like public shaming rituals, the play places the female bodies of Kate, Bianca, and the widow on display and by not returning to Sly relaxes the frame and "allows the audience to forget that Petruchio's taming of Kate is presented as a fiction." Yet the containment of woman is troubled, for on the Elizabethan and Jacobean stage women were played by boys. Thus the play's "patriarchal master narrative" is undermined.

Novy, Marianne. "Patriarchy and Play in *The Taming of the Shrew.*" *English Literary Renaissance* 9 (1979): 264–80.

For Novy, *The Taming of the Shrew* combines patriarchy and companionship in its picture of marriage. Although Petruchio's initiative is consistent with patriarchy, the frequent references to hierarchy and tradition are often "undercut by their use as a pretext for self-assertion." Novy finds an analog for the companionate marriage in historical evidence from Elizabethan England that shows increased desire for companionship in its ideals of marriage.

Stallybrass, Peter. "Patriarchal Territories: The Body Enclosed." In *Rewriting the Renaissance: The Discourse of Sexual Difference in Early Modern Europe,* edited by Margaret W. Ferguson, Maureen Quilligan, and Nancy Vickers, pp. 123–42. Chicago: University of Chicago Press, 1986.

Stallybrass provides a broad overview of Renaissance definitions of women as a category of male property that required women to be silent and chaste. Unlike their medieval predecessors, Renaissance women of all classes were increasingly confined to a private sphere. Although the enclosure of the female body in the Renaissance was often defined by humanist writers with reference to ancient households of Greece and Rome, Stallybrass shows that it was a product of specific socioeconomic changes and new canons of "polite behavior."

Underdown, David. "The Taming of the Scold: The Enforcement of Patriarchal Authority in Early Modern England." In *Order and Disorder in Early Modern England*, pp. 116–35. Cambridge: Cambridge University Press, 1985.

According to Underdown, fears of an impending breakdown in the established patriarchal social order were widespread in early modern England. This anxiety displayed itself in a vast literature rife with reference to rebellious wives and hectored husbands. In order to determine whether this "threat" to the social order was real or imagined, Underdown sketches a historical context of disobedient wives, rising accusations of witchcraft, and single women refusing to enter service. After gathering evidence, Underdown concludes that the "literary and sub-literary works" touching the topic, including Shakespeare's *Taming of the Shrew*, were provoked by a "period of strained gender relations in early modern England."

Underdown, David. *Revel, Riot and Rebellion: Popular Politics and Culture in England 1603–1660*. New York: Oxford University Press, 1985.

Underdown sets out to describe the behavior of the English common people (that is, people below the gentry rank) during the civil wars and revolutions of 1640–60 and then to account for some of the changing standards of behavior after the Restoration in 1660. Underdown finds a decrease in the prosecution of scolds and witches after 1660 and declares that "after 1688 patriarchy lost much of its credibility as a theory of government." He attributes this shift to changing economic conditions and a more humane model of family relationships.

Wayne, Valerie. "Refashioning the Shrew." *Shakespeare Studies* 17 (1985): 159–87.

Considering the role of the shrew in the drama of the Wakefield Master and William Shakespeare, Wayne purposes to show how two of the "best medieval and Renaissance writers" could use the shrew to raise issues about women and marriage without endorsing the brutal attitudes expressed toward shrews in the playwrights' age. For while the character of the shrew arose from a patriarchal society, she was also the best means of calling into question the prevailing power structure when kings or husbands misused their authority.

Shakespeare's Language

Abbott, E. A. *A Shakespearian Grammar*. New York: Haskell House, 1972.

This compact reference book, first published in 1870, helps with many difficulties in Shakespeare's language. It systematically accounts for a host of differences between Shakespeare's usage and sentence structure and our own.

Blake, Norman. *Shakespeare's Language: An Introduction*. New York: St. Martin's Press, 1983.

This general introduction to Elizabethan English discusses various aspects of the language of Shakespeare and his contemporaries, offering possible meanings for hundreds of ambiguous constructions.

Dobson, E. J. *English Pronunciation, 1500–1700*. 2 vols. Oxford: Clarendon Press, 1968.

This long and technical work includes chapters on spelling (and its reformation), phonetics, stressed vowels, and consonants in early modern English.

Houston, John. *Shakespearean Sentences: A Study in Style and Syntax*. Baton Rouge: Louisiana State University Press, 1988.

Houston studies Shakespeare's stylistic choices, considering matters such as sentence length and the relative positions of subject, verb, and direct object. Examining plays throughout the canon in a roughly chronological, developmental order, he analyzes how sentence structure is used in setting tone, in characterization, and for other dramatic purposes.

Onions, C. T. *A Shakespeare Glossary*. Oxford: Clarendon Press, 1986.

This revised edition updates Onions's standard, selective glossary of words and phrases in Shakespeare's plays that are now obsolete, archaic, or obscure.

Partridge, Eric. *Shakespeare's Bawdy*. London: Routledge & Kegan Paul, 1955.

After an introductory essay, "The Sexual, the Homosexual, and Non-Sexual Bawdy in Shakespeare," Partridge provides a comprehensive glossary of "bawdy" phrases and words from the plays.

Robinson, Randal. *Unlocking Shakespeare's Language: Help for the Teacher and Student*. Urbana, Ill.: National Council of Teachers of English and the ERIC Clearinghouse on Reading and Communication Skills, 1989.

Specifically designed for the high-school and undergraduate college teacher and student, Robinson's book addresses the problems that most often hinder present-day readers of Shakespeare. Through work with his own students, Robinson found that many readers today are particularly puzzled by such stylistic characteristics as subject-verb inversion, interrupted structures, and compression. He shows how our own colloquial language contains comparable structures, and thus helps students recognize such structures when they find them in Shakespeare's plays. This book supplies worksheets— with examples from major plays—to illuminate and remedy such problems as unusual sequences of words and the separation of related parts of sentences.

Shakespeare's Life

Baldwin, T. W. *William Shakspere's Petty School*. Urbana: University of Illinois Press, 1943.

Baldwin here investigates the theory and practice of the petty school, the first level of education in Elizabethan England. He focuses on that educational system primarily as it is reflected in Shakespeare's art.

Baldwin, T. W. *William Shakspere's Small Latine and Lesse Greeke*. 2 vols. Urbana: University of Illinois Press, 1944.

Baldwin attacks the view that Shakespeare was an uneducated genius—a view that had been dominant among Shakespeareans since the eighteenth century. Instead, Baldwin shows, the educational system of Shakespeare's time would have given the playwright a strong background in the classics, and there is much in the plays that shows how Shakespeare benefited from such an education.

Beier, A. L., and Roger Finlay, eds. *London 1500–1800: The Making of the Metropolis*. New York: Longman, 1986.

Focusing on the economic and social history of early modern London, these collected essays probe aspects of metropolitan life, including "Population and Disease," "Commerce and Manufacture," and "Society and Change."

Bentley, G. E. *Shakespeare's Life: A Biographical Handbook.* New Haven: Yale University Press, 1961.
This "just-the-facts" account presents the surviving documents of Shakespeare's life against an Elizabethan background.

Chambers, E. K. *William Shakespeare: A Study of Facts and Problems.* 2 vols. Oxford: Clarendon Press, 1930.
Analyzing in great detail the scant historical data, Chambers's complex, scholarly study considers the nature of the texts in which Shakespeare's work is preserved.

Cressy, David. *Education in Tudor and Stuart England.* London: Edward Arnold, 1975.
This volume collects sixteenth-, seventeenth-, and early-eighteenth-century documents detailing aspects of formal education in England, such as the curriculum, the control and organization of education, and the education of women.

Dutton, Richard. *William Shakespeare: A Literary Life.* New York: St. Martin's Press, 1989.
Not a biography in the traditional sense, Dutton's very readable work nevertheless "follows the contours of Shakespeare's life" as he examines Shakespeare's career as playwright and poet, with consideration of his patrons, theatrical associations, and audience.

Fraser, Russell. *Young Shakespeare.* New York: Columbia University Press, 1988.
Fraser focuses on Shakespeare's first thirty years, paying attention simultaneously to his life and art.

De Grazia, Margreta. *Shakespeare Verbatim: The Reproduction of Authenticity and the Apparatus of 1790.* Oxford: Clarendon Press, 1991.

De Grazia traces and discusses the development of such editorial criteria as authenticity, historical periodization, factual biography, chronological developments, and close reading, locating as the point of origin Edmond Malone's 1790 edition of Shakespeare's works. There are interesting chapters on the First Folio and on the "legendary" versus the "documented" Shakespeare.

Schoenbaum, S. *William Shakespeare: A Compact Documentary Life.* New York: Oxford University Press, 1977.
This standard biography economically presents the essential documents from Shakespeare's time in an accessible narrative account of the playwright's life.

Shakespeare's Theater

Bentley, G. E. *The Profession of Player in Shakespeare's Time, 1590–1642.* Princeton: Princeton University Press, 1984.
Bentley readably sets forth a wealth of evidence about performance in Shakespeare's time, with special attention to the relations between player and company, and the business of casting, managing, and touring.

Berry, Herbert. *Shakespeare's Playhouses.* New York: AMS Press, 1987.
Berry's six essays collected here discuss (with illustrations) varying aspects of the four playhouses in which Shakespeare had a financial stake: the Theatre in Shoreditch, the Blackfriars, and the first and second Globe.

Cook, Ann Jennalie. *The Privileged Playgoers of Shakespeare's London*. Princeton: Princeton University Press, 1981.

Cook's work argues, on the basis of sociological, economic, and documentary evidence, that Shakespeare's audience—and the audience for English Renaissance drama generally—consisted mainly of the "privileged."

Greg, W. W. *Dramatic Documents from the Elizabethan Playhouses*. 2 vols. Oxford: Clarendon Press, 1931.

Greg itemizes and briefly describes almost all the play manuscripts that survive from the period 1590 to around 1660, including, among other things, players' parts. His second volume offers facsimiles of selected manuscripts.

Gurr, Andrew. *Playgoing in Shakespeare's London*. Cambridge: Cambridge University Press, 1987.

Gurr charts how the theatrical enterprise developed from its modest beginnings in the late 1560s to become a thriving institution in the 1600s. He argues that there were important changes over the period 1567–1644 in the playhouses, the audience, and the plays.

Harbage, Alfred. *Shakespeare's Audience*. New York: Columbia University Press, 1941.

Harbage investigates the fragmentary surviving evidence to interpret the size, composition, and behavior of Shakespeare's audience.

Hattaway, Michael. *Elizabethan Popular Theatre: Plays in Performance*. London: Routledge & Kegan Paul, 1982.

Beginning with a study of the popular drama of the

late Elizabethan age—a description of the stages, performance conditions, and acting of the period—this volume concludes with an analysis of five well-known plays of the 1590s, one of them (*Titus Andronicus*) by Shakespeare.

Shapiro, Michael. *Children of the Revels: The Boy Companies of Shakespeare's Time and Their Plays.* New York: Columbia University Press, 1977.

Shapiro chronicles the history of the amateur and quasi-professional child companies that flourished in London at the end of Elizabeth's reign and the beginning of James's.

The Publication of Shakespeare's Plays

Blayney, Peter. *The First Folio of Shakespeare.* Hanover, Md.: Folger, 1991.

Blayney's accessible account of the printing and later life of the First Folio—an amply illustrated catalogue to a 1991 Folger Shakespeare Library exhibition—analyzes the mechanical production of the First Folio, describing how the Folio was made, by whom and for whom, how much it cost, and its ups and downs (or, rather, downs and ups) since its printing in 1623.

Hinman, Charlton. *The Printing and Proof-Reading of the First Folio of Shakespeare.* 2 vols. Oxford: Clarendon Press, 1963.

In the most arduous study of a single book ever undertaken, Hinman attempts to reconstruct how the Shakespeare First Folio of 1623 was set into type and run off the press, sheet by sheet. He also provides almost all the known variations in readings from copy to copy.

Hinman, Charlton. *The Norton Facsimile: The First Folio of Shakespeare.* New York: W. W. Norton, 1968.

This facsimile presents a photographic reproduction of an "ideal" copy of the First Folio of Shakespeare; Hinman attempts to represent each page in its most fully corrected state.

Key to
Famous Lines and Phrases

No profit grows where is no pleasure ta'en.
In brief, sir, study what you most affect.

[Tranio—1.1.39–40]

I come to wive it wealthy in Padua;
If wealthily, then happily in Padua.

[Petruchio—1.2.76–77]

. . . nothing comes amiss, so money comes withal.

[Grumio—1.2.83]

Old fashions please me best.   [Bianca—3.1.83]

Who wooed in haste and means to wed at leisure.

[Katherine—3.2.11]

This is a way to kill a wife with kindness.

[Petruchio—4.1.208]

Our purses shall be proud, our garments poor,
For 'tis the mind that makes the body rich . . .

[Petruchio—4.3.177–78]